DISCOVERING MY SOUTHERN LEGACY

Deirdre Foreman

DISCOVERING MY SOUTHERN LEGACY

Slave Culture and the American South

The Black Studies Collection

Collection Editor
Dr Chris McAuley

LPP

First published in 2024 by Lived Places Publishing.

The authors and editors have made every effort to ensure the accuracy of information contained in this publication, but assume no responsibility for any errors, inaccuracies, inconsistencies or omissions. Likewise, every effort has been made to contact copyright holders. If any copyright material has been reproduced unwittingly and without permission the Publisher will gladly receive information enabling them to rectify any error or omission in subsequent editions.

British Library Cataloguing in Publication Data
A CIP record for this book is available from the British Library

ISBN: 9781915271662 (pbk)
ISBN: 9781915271686 (ePDF)
ISBN: 9781915271679 (ePUB)

The right of Deirdre Foreman to be identified as the Author of this work has been asserted by her in accordance with the Copyright, Design and Patents Act 1988.

Cover design by Fiachra McCarthy
Book design by Rachel Trolove of Twin Trail Design
Typeset by Newgen Publishing UK

Lived Places Publishing
Long Island
New York 11789

www.livedplacespublishing.com

Abstract

In this book, the author explores the cultural legacy of enslaved Africans in the American South through an ethnoautobiographical reflection of her own African American identity and family heritage. Through storytelling and personal narratives, the author describes her family's cultural practices and how they are directly rooted in those of the enslaved Africans on the Southern plantation. Known as "cultural survivors," enslaved Africans established cultural customs and norms out of resistance to the control of white slaveholders to maintain their independence and pride. Scholars purport that slave culture is an "Afro-American culture"—a blend of Africa and America. Unwittingly, the author's family has practiced the culture of enslaved Africans for generations. African culture, which has historically been viewed as inferior to "European" culture, is influential in many American families. However, it has largely gone unexamined.

This book highlights the author's travels to Ghana, West Africa, a depot for the transatlantic slave trade, as an inspiration for her journey to learn more about West African culture and her family's connection to West African traditions. The author reveals how she has come full circle by returning to the continent where it all began. In the Appendix, the author presents a multidimensional explanatory model of the African American identity from slavery to modern-day oppression.

By writing this book, the author seeks to connect Africa to her own family heritage in honor of her enslaved ancestors to heal the pain from the generational traumas suffered throughout the African diaspora.

Keywords

Ethnoautobiography, African American, Black studies, Black history, antebellum, slave culture, racism, slavery, family, ancestry

Contents

Acknowledgments

I acknowledge and dedicate this book to my enslaved African ancestors who suffered the pain of the transatlantic slave trade and enslavement worldwide. In America, they left behind a legacy of Southern traditions and customs that are influential in my family and have contributed to the acculturation of many American families. Their legacy has provided a sense of racial and cultural identity for many Black families. Their contributions to African American history and culture give us a sense of belonging and connect us to the Motherland. Without their creations, our people would not have been able to sustain racial and cultural independence.

I thank my family, who continue to support me in academic and career endeavors. To all those who never doubted my ability to achieve success, I thank you. Thank you to family members who are eager to share their stories of our family legacy. I hope that this book serves as an inspiration to those who are in search of the cultural legacy of enslaved Africans in America.

Notes on language and content

Content warning: Every effort has been made to provide more specific content warnings before relevant chapters, but please be aware that references to potentially distressing topics occur frequently and throughout the book.

Explicit references: This book contains explicit references to, and descriptions of, situations that may cause distress, as well as language that some may find distressing. This includes words such as enslavement, slavery, and white indentured servitude.

Capitalization: Black is capitalized but not white—denoting that Black culture can be considered a diverse but cohesive community with a shared experience of historical and ongoing systemic oppression. In contrast, white cultures and communities lack this shared experience and therefore lack the same kind of cultural cohesiveness as a wider group.

Cultural language: The author uses "African American vs. Black" to highlight the historical and cultural connection of American-born Black to Africa.

Objective language: The author uses slavery/enslavement language or person-first language such as "enslaved person" to push back against the concept of the slave as an object and brings to the front of mind that these people were/are people, first and foremost. Slave objectifies and dehumanizes the individual.

Introduction

In this book, I explore the cultural legacy of enslaved Africans in the American South through an ethnoautobiographical reflection of my African American identity and my family's cultural heritage. My travels to Ghana inspired me to learn more about my connection to Africa. I have discovered that much of my cultural heritage is rooted in that of enslaved Africans as it was practiced on the Southern plantation. Enslaved Africans, during European colonization, developed their own system of rituals and habits that produced core values and beliefs among the kinships formed on the Southern plantation to maintain cultural independence in plantation life. These traditions, which are extremely influential in the acculturation of my family, include the plantation quarters, tobacco farming, gardening, "emotional" religion and superstition, family support and cooperation, and hair customs (Blassingame, 1979).

The enslaved had strong West African oral traditions of prayer, song, lament, and storytelling (Washington, 1899), all of which my family unwittingly practiced for generations. Another tradition, such as the Southern drawl, which is more animated than common English, is prevalent across the American South and in my family. Rhythmic music rooted in West African tradition provides for energetic dances at family celebrations and church services. For the enslaved, in religious settings, music was the power behind the prayer, and dance was the expression of the sound (Blassingame, 1979). Music sustained rhythms for the enslaved during times of hard labor; it spread across the Southern plantation and throughout the slave community (Chase, 1970). On board slave ships during the Middle Passage, captured Africans were forced to dance and entertain the slave traders (Du Bois, 1903).

Despite the dehumanization and modern-day oppression that the enslaved and their descendants have experienced throughout history, we as a people take pride in and pass on our cultural traditions as my family has done for generations. The historical literature indicates that African slave culture is American culture.

Joseph E. Holloway (2005), a major contributor to diasporic studies, in *Africanisms in American Culture,* provided a historical analysis of the cultural contributions of enslaved Africans in the American South. He studied the cultural history of Africans in the New World during one of the most critical points in American history, when the development of the cultural history of what it means to be an American was questioned. Building on the theories of Melville J. Herskovits (1938), known as the father of "New World African" studies, Holloway has offered a series of essays on the African cultural survivals that have evolved throughout American slavery, Jim Crow, and modern-day racial discrimination. Furthermore, he examined African cultural traditions that are practiced in America, such as names, foods, religion, and music.

Sheila S. Walker (2001), in her book *African Roots/American Cultures,* highlighted Africans and their descendants who populated the majority of the modern Americas for the first 300 years of their five centuries of existence. Yet their contributions to the creation and the definition of what we would describe as "American society" to the New World, and their significance in the development of the African diaspora, have been omitted from the history books. Walker (2001) underscored the African presence throughout the Americas, Africa, and the African diasporic world from a historical perspective, capturing the contributions made to all of the Americas. Her compilation of short essays from an array of scholars and cultural anthropologists from African diasporic communities are enlightening.

In this book, *Discovering My Southern Legacy: Slave Culture and the American South,* I present a multidimensional African American cultural identity model from slavery to modern-day oppression. This model includes discussions on American slavery, internal colonization and colonialism, Noel and Blauner's (1968) hypothesis on minority group status, paternalism, oppositional culture, double consciousness, the theory of racism proposed by Brondolo et al. (2012) and Jones (1997), and Bourdieu's theory of social reproduction. Culture—a set of beliefs, ideas, and values passed down from generation to generation—is central to this study.

According to Smedley and Smedley (2012), the notion that African Americans are of a race inferior to that of Europeans and that, therefore, African culture is inferior to European culture, has been the racial worldview for centuries. The cultural revelations that are discussed in this book are confirmations, disclosures, and divulgences that construct a bridge to my enslaved ancestors who were brought by force from the Motherland to the New World. Vital to my existence is the acceptance that, throughout my lifetime, I have lived in a society that is historically racially and culturally oppressed and overwhelmed by cultural violence in the form of cultural racism. As a descendant of slaves, I am part of a colonized minority group who were brought to the Americas through involuntary migration. This history defines my experiences of the denial and suppression of African ancestral contributions to American society.

To understand my family legacy, I offer a captivating explanatory model of the African American cultural and racial identity. "American culture" does not exist without acknowledgment of enslaved Africans in America. This book challenges any notion that "Afro-American culture" is inferior to any other culture.

1
Ghana

In this chapter we explore the author's travels to Ghana and her discovery of the truth behind the transatlantic slave trade and West African customs and traditions.

Learning objectives

- To gain broader awareness of common West African cultural tradition and American culture.
- To gain a broader perspective of the author's purpose for this study and her spiritual connection to Africa.
- To expand knowledge of Ghana's historical sites that contributed to the transatlantic slave trade.

My journey to learn more about my connection to the Motherland begins with my travels to Ghana, West Africa. Through this life-changing travel experience, I immersed myself in West African culture, such as foods, farming, dress, and hairstyles. While visiting the many sites that were once occupied by enslaved Africans who were transported to the New World during the transatlantic slave trade, I have come to the realization that there is nothing more important than honoring my ancestors for their contributions in shaping who I am as an African American woman in America. Through genealogical research, I found that Ghana is a part of my ancestry.

I arrive at the Kotoka International Airport in the center of the city of Accra. As I step off the plane, I peek out of the aircraft service door to see the wonders before me. I step down to the tarmac and think to myself, "This is PARADISE! This is HOME!" The sun gives me a happy feeling. The air, with the fresh smell of saltwater, serves as a healing potion to many on the continent. I exit the plane and notice someone looking up at me. A woman awaits, wearing a white blouse and a navy-blue skirt. She smiles and then extends her hand to offer me assistance. My steps down the stairs symbolize the transition from the cultural oppression that I feel in the United States to my anticipated cultural freedom in West Africa. I am confronted with feelings of exhilaration and nervousness. Exhilaration because I am ecstatic finally to have arrived in the Motherland and nervous because, as an African American in West Africa, I do not know what to expect. I hop onto the airport shuttle bus; off to the airport entrance we go!

Being here, a "foreigner" in a "familiar" land, makes me uneasy at first. However, as the day progresses, the feelings of uncertainty slowly dissipate.

When I enter through the sliding glass doors of the airport, I hear the rhythmic percussive sounds of the African drum. Like most of my soul "sistas" would do, I move my hips and bop my head to the beat. The Ghanaian musical performers play the African drums, the Kpanlogo, and hand beat the Ewe drums. Although I am not an expert, I identify the sounds as the popular music in Ghana called "Highlife." My friend and colleague share the history behind the sound, which originated in the Gold Coast during the colonial days of the 1900s and combines many West African rhythms, such as Northern and Black American musicals, as well as swing, and jazz, into one sound known as "*soukous*." The music permeates my soul. The beats make me feel connected to the Motherland. Before I reach my hotel destination, I experience the wonders of Ghana. I react to musical sounds that I have never felt before. As I listen to the rhythmic patterns, with drummers seemingly improvising new sounds, I disengage my book bag from my shoulder, tap my feet, and move my hips as if I were doing the hula hoop twist in the front yard of my great-grandparent's home affectionally known as the "Big House" yard. Little Black girls back in the United States know what I am talking about, with the hula hoop. As a child, I used to play with the hula hoop almost daily after school. I see a female Ghanaian dancer wearing braids, a West African tradition. She is wearing an instrument around her waist like the hula hoop. The history of the hula hoop begins in Egypt as far back as 3000 BCE, when the Egyptians were "curving reeds and rattan into circles" for their children to play with and swing around their waists or push with wooden sticks or toss into the air (Vogan, 2022).

While in Ghana, I am reminded of my childhood in southern Virginia, where my family resides. As we drive across the countryside from the city of Accra to Kumasi, a city in the Ashanti region, I see rural villages that look like my family's home in Brookneal, Virginia. I see farm animals, large and small—cows, horses, goats, chickens—all along the farmland. The scent of horse manure permeates the air, igniting the same annoyed response that I have on my family farm in Virginia. I hold my nose until the stench subsides, and I think, "Wow, this is just like the [country]." (A term of endearment that we (my family) use to describe the American South.)

Ghanaians are walking on the street, barefoot with pride, as if they are wearing invisible golden slippers. This African custom has been passed down for generations in my family. When I was a little girl, around the age of 10, we jumped rope and played barefoot. This was one of my favorite pastimes. But of course, at that young age, my social awareness and Black consciousness had not yet developed with regard to my ancestral connection to Africa. I was not able to make the cultural connection to my enslaved African culture. There are roosters everywhere, black and white, crowing as they wander along the road, seemingly in search of their flock. Back in Virginia on our family farm, we built a hen house for hens and roosters to reside with cockerels and baby chicks. Similarly, it appears that in Ghana poultry are valued stock on the farm.

The houses along the long road are seemingly miles apart, as are those in my family's neighborhood in rural Virginia. The town in which my maternal grandmother, Cathy, resided, known as Red House, looks like an African village. Acres and acres of land, isolated residences. Long fenced-in farms, with green grass and red dirt. In Ghana, one house in particular catches my eye as we drive past. Several barefoot children are sitting on the porch. The scene reminds me of my cousins, and in my mind I am sitting on the porch at my great-grandmother's residence, the "Big House."

I listen to the musical sounds that are like the sounds of African beads and shakers, with an African rhythm. Not knowing the proper West African dance moves, I improvise. I am comforted by the musician's warm smiles. Suddenly, I hear finger popping and hands clapping from the accidental audience. Traditional music in most of the continent is passed down orally (or aurally) and is not written (Finkelman, 1989). This experience is not only a cultural revelation but also a musical celebration of my journey.

After hundreds of years and millions of slave descendants before me, I have come full circle to return to where it all began. In Ghana, I experience community and cultural exchange throughout the country. I am visiting the Nungua fishing villages, Jamestown, and Kumasi. Engaging in impactful activities promotes cultural exchange and understanding between visitors and members of the community. To become better acquainted with West African culture, I engaged the Nungua fishing village community that hosts batik artists, potters, native Kente fabric artists, basket weavers, musicians and dancers, and many others who contribute to the distinctive character of the village.

I explored several sites in English-speaking and non-English-speaking communities throughout West Africa to enhance my knowledge of West African traditions. I visited the University of Cape Coast, the University of Ghana, Kintampo Waterfalls, Kakum Park, and historical sites such as the W. E. B. Du Bois Memorial Center for Pan African Culture, Cape Coast Castle, Elmina Castle, and the Kwame Nkrumah Mausoleum. I visited the Kwame Nkrumah University of Science and Technology (also known as KNUST), the largest university in the Kumasi metropolis and the Ashanti region. In Kumasi (the middle of the nation), the ancestral home of the Ashanti Empire that ruled what is now central Ghana from the seventeenth through the nineteenth centuries, until the advent of British colonialism, I engage in a fact-finding project to discover the rise of the Ashanti Empire and the source of spiritual strength that unified them as a nation.

The transatlantic slave trade—the shipment of Africans to Europe, the Caribbean islands, South America, and British North America—was critical in developing the slave plantation in the American south. I reflect on this as I walk through the Castle of St. George at Elmina, known as "Elmina Castle," overlooking the "Bight of Benin" on Ghana's West African Gold Coast. In this book, the "Elmina Castle" will be referred to as the "Elmina dungeon," based on the history of atrocities that took place there. Erected by the Portuguese in 1482, this structure was once a fortress for many European countries such as the British, Dutch, Swedes, Portuguese, and Germans who built their financial empires based on the slave trade (Bruner, 1996).

Known to be the oldest European constructed slave dungeon, this cracked and faded edifice is nestled in the midst of this coastal Ghanaian community. It is surrounded by a population of native Ghanaians with limited knowledge of its history. The deficiency of African history in the Ghanaian educational curriculum is based on native testimony and is an area that needs further examination.

Stationed along the shores, Ghana's shameful history contradicts its grandeur. I peer out over the edge of the balcony of the Elmina slave dungeon; I can see where the slave ships once docked to load the human cargo for shipment to what would become the African diaspora. I doubt whether anyone could ever completely comprehend the feeling. The horrors of this history produce for me both anxiety and sadness. Here, I learn about the historical events that stripped any human dignity from my ancestors as they were led into a world of uncertainty and darkness. I realize at that moment that I am a lost child at sea.

An empty vessel with nothing to offer except tears of sorrow. I reflect on the pain that my ancestors must have endured and contemplate the long-term effects on my psyche. This visit is impactful and inspires me to learn more about my connection to Africa. This encounter confirms the need to build a bridge of healing from the generational traumas of the past. Highlighting the contributions of enslaved African people in the United States helps me to achieve this goal.

I enter the doorway of the Elmina slave dungeon. An indescribable emotion overcomes me. In the cold and darkness, I see flowers placed on the cement floors by tourists as a makeshift memorial to our ancestors. The tour guide instructs us to cover our heads for protection against the bat webs in the corners of the ceilings. However, I have no fear, for those webs represent for me time and place: time, as in the years that continue to pass, even as the stain of this history remains, and place, where the naked bodies of my ancestors lie.

I try to leave, but I cannot. Despite the chill in the air and the sound of the speaker's voice insisting that I leave this sacred space, I cannot move. I am enthralled by the stench that permeates the air. I hear the cries of screaming voices, begging for their lives. The smell of blood and feces from centuries ago still lingers in the air. The cold stone walls engulf me. I can barely breathe. All I can think about are my ancestors who were stolen from their village and shipped off.

European trading posts for African life contributed to the mass enslavement of African people. The northern British colonies, later to become North America, created a system of enslavement quite different from that of Africa and other places in the world.

The American system of slavery was chattel slavery. Bondage for life. Humans as property. Damage to a people that nobody could have ever imagined. Every step that I take is slow and heavy, as if the spirits have entered my body and beg me to stay in the "female dungeon," where enslaved women were kept for not submitting to the sexual demands of their captors.

The speaker recites the English names given to Africans held captive in the dungeon. Adams. Brown. Whitefield. Fenwick. Thomas. Williams. Clark. Johnson. The European slave officials and traders resided in large luxury suites with "master" bedrooms, dining rooms, and meeting rooms located on the upper level of the slave dungeon while facilitating the entrapment of Africans for economic power and control (Prayag, Suntikul, and Agyeiwaah, 2018) I know at this moment that this is real. The African American connection to Africa is real. Here I stand, an African American woman, born and raised in the United States of America. I ask, what does this all mean?

My descendants were stolen from this land. Ripped from the bosom of the Motherland. The tears roll down my face; I cannot stop them. I cry a drop for every lash of the whip that my ancestors took in this space. I will remain until I am done. I now know my mission. My life has changed forever.

2
The "Big House"

In this chapter we learn about the historical significance of the "Big House" on the Southern plantation.

Learning objectives

- To broaden awareness of the "Big House" as a central role in the establishment of racial casting on the Southern plantation.
- To examine how race and science were inextricably linked to Black oppression.
- To learn culinary practices of the enslaved African common to African American Southern culture.
- To learn about the "Big House" as a cultural custom in the author's family heritage.

In Virginia, our two-story family home, situated on 500 acres, is affectionately known as the "Big House." The term "Big House" is directly rooted in the history of antebellum slavery, as it is the term that enslaved Africans used for the home of the plantation owner (Finkelman, 1989). The "Big House" is central to my family ancestry. For my family, it represents the connection to the legacy of enslaved Africans on the Southern plantation.

In 1899, 34 years after ratification of the Thirteenth Amendment, which legally "freed" all slaves in the United States, my great-great-grandfather purchased a small cabin for $100 on 48.75

acres of the land that he had inherited from his employer, a white tobacco plantation owner. This cabin was on that land until about 1904. In 1910 the value had increased to $168, but by 1913 it had mysteriously decreased to $111. In 1911, my great-great-grandfather inherited another 146.25 acres from the same white plantation owner. He built a small house there. In 1920, he willed the land and house to his "suspected" son, my great-grandfather, at which time the property value had increased to $200.

Great-grandpa was a beacon of the local community. His vision for the land expanded beyond what was considered achievable for African Americans during that time period. In 1935, he borrowed $350 from a bank to build what is known in our family as the "Big House." This begins the legacy of the "Big House" in my family ancestry. My great-grandfather and great-grandmother moved into the "Big House" in 1938 after they were married and raised eight children there. In Brookneal, Virginia, the "Big House" is the symbol of domesticity and tobacco farming within the community. Located about one mile down the road from my maternal grandmother's house, the "Big House" stands alone, with few surrounding properties except for the cabin quarters where my great-grandfather housed his sharecroppers. He employed several African American sharecroppers in the surrounding areas and across the state. On weekdays, they would come to work the field and sleep in the cabins on the property, then leave every Friday afternoon for the weekend.

Rumor has it that my great-grandfather's biological father is the son of a white plantation owner. This explains perhaps why his "father" inherited so much land and why he was revered in the community. This was unusual for the time. His very fair skin and rumored parentage, although never confirmed, provided him with privileges that were not afforded to most Blacks during that time. "It was generally assumed throughout the slave period by both whites and Blacks that mulattoes were superior in intelligence to pure Blacks" (Finkelman, 1989, p. 134). During this time, race and science were inextricably linked to Black oppression. The use of race as a method of social differentiation and human variation is a recent phenomenon.

Historical records indicate that the concepts associated with race became more popular after the seventeenth century (Dennis, 1995; Foreman, 2017; Smedley, 1998). As early as the nineteenth century, scientific racism acquired and maintained global dominance (Dennis, 1995; Foreman, 2017; Smedley, 1998). It meant that, based on conclusions drawn in scientific methodology, Black Americans were an inferior race, compared to peoples of European ancestry. This theory not only served as a basis for racial casting and social division; but it also spearheaded the idea that Blacks were an inferior race. However, when linked to scientific inquiry, this claim is indisputably unproven (Dennis, 1995; Foreman, 2017; Smedley, 1998). For example, as advanced by Foreman (2017, p. 74), the book entitled *The Scholar Denied: W.E.B. Du Bois and the Birth of Modern Sociology,* written by Aldon Morris, is a framework that highlights Du Bois as a scientific sociologist who rejected racist scientific claims and developed the intellectual philosophy on how social factors, not biology, explained the "Negro problem" in America. Foreman (2017) highlighted Morris's (2015) revelations on Du Bois's fieldwork research methods conducted at the Du Bois–Atlanta

School to refute these claims. According to Morris (2015, cited in Foreman, 2017):

> The investigative tools of the Du Bois-Atlanta school encompassed surveys, interviews, participant observations, organizational documents, and census data. These were empirical techniques that the first generation of black students undergoing graduate training in white universities wanted to master. Through such means, they believed, crucial data for overwhelming racial ignorance and stereotypes would be gathered.
>
> (Foreman, 2017, p. 36)

Further analysis, as advanced by Foreman (2017, p. 36) on Morris's (2015) research, is that Du Bois studied communities, observed how Blacks lived in their environment, and methodically collected data that aided in developing the foundation of his social scientific theories on racial inferiority. Furthermore, according to Morris (2015, as cited in Foreman, 2017, p. 36), Du Bois, known as the founding father of this type of research method, applied it to many of his studies, such as "The Philadelphia Negro," "The Negroes of Farmville," and many others that he conducted at the Atlanta school.

The categorization of human beings into distinct groupings, based on physical characteristics and intellectual abilities, prompted among scientists the supposition that Black Americans were "in the throes of a degenerative evolutionary process" (Brandt, 1978, p. 21) and were inferior to the white race (Dennis, 1995; Foreman, 2017; Smedley, 1998).

The "Big House" looks like something out of a children's pop-up story book. It has gray wood shingles, a bronze tin roof, and a large back porch that serves as the main entrance. It has three bedrooms—one on the first floor and two on the second floor—and a living room and dining room. The "Big House" has a small kitchen inside the house with a wood stove, and a basement with a dirt floor that was used as a coolant area for fruits and vegetables grown in the garden. There is an outhouse in the back yard that was used before plumbing was installed in the house. When my mother was a child, one used a chamber pot at night in frigid weather. There are wood stoves in the kitchen, dining room, living room, and every bedroom. There is no thermostat, so the house was cold in winter and hot in summer. There is a cut-out or hole with a handle on the stove to adjust the temperature so the wood would not burn fast. The wood was kept by the stove. Even in snow, we had to get the wood from outside. We used oil lanterns with a glass top and wick all through the house. The wick controls the brightness of the light resonating from the lamp. Owing to limited electricity in the house, oil lanterns had to be carried from room to room. My mother shared with me that the electricity was installed in the house prior to the indoor plumbing for the bathroom. In the tobacco house, we used the oil lanterns to see when tying up the tobacco.

A space for family meal gatherings, communal prayer, and religious celebrations, the "Big House" gleams in the sunlight like a castle on the hill. Also known as the "planter's residence," the "Big House" "was the most prominent building by virtue of its size and position and occasionally was adorned with stylish architectural features" (Moore, 2009, p. 67). It remains the prime icon of plantation identity. As the home of the white plantation owner, the "Big House" set the tone for the plantation. Its historical foundation bore the burden of grief and pain for the field workers for generations as the plantation owner used it to create a racial caste system on the plantation.

During slavery, the "Big House" was the main source of fragmentation in the slave community. Labor divisions based on the responsibilities of the enslaved dictated the nature of the relationship of the slaveholder with the enslaved. The Southern plantation was the place where the enslaved were divided for "purposes of labor" into house or field workers (Finkelman, 1989). Only the fair-skinned domesticated slaves worked in the "Big House." The field was reserved for the lower-class enslaved, or the "brutes," "laborers," "liars," "parasites," or "thieves" (Finkelman, 1989).

Domestic servants assimilated more easily with the white plantation owners owing to their proximity to the white Southern elite class. However, despite this slight accorded privilege, the enslaved knew their place in the social hierarchy. Known as the "Black aristocrats," the enslaved African domestic servants were viewed as "superior" in intelligence to the enslaved workers in the field (Finkelman, 1989; Harper, 1985). This caste system created a culture of social divisions among the slaves on the plantation that affected the African American community for generations. European culture has historically been favored in American society. As Harper (1985) noted, "Without doubt, domestic servants absorbed more white culture than other slaves, but this was partially because domestics were selected for qualities which advanced that process" (p. 124).

In 1966, after great-grandpa Robert passed away, great-grandma Lene (I called her Grandma Lene) lived in the "Big House" with her twin sons and nephew until her death in 1977.

Childhood memory

Momma and I drive to the "Big House" to pay Grandma Lene a visit. As we approach the house, I see the tobacco fields, Great-Uncle Jeffrey's brick house, and cousin Harry's trailers. I see it ever so clearly. The "Big House" looks like a mansion. We pull the car into the yard. I see Grandma Lene sitting on the porch in her favorite rocking chair, finally taking a rest from her cooking, cleaning, laundry, ironing, and gardening. These are her favorite things to do. Taking care of the family is her priority. She wipes the sweat from her brow.

There is no driveway, only dirt and grass in the yard. She glances up and sees us approach the house. She stands all of 5'2" tall, waving us into the yard and smiling with those pretty pearly white teeth. Born in 1897, roughly 30 years after the abolition of slavery and 20 years after the Reconstruction era, Grandma Lene lived a life not far removed from slavery. In retrospect, the cultural influences that she shared with my family are reflective of the recent history of the enslaved within her lifetime.

At the tender age of 78, she is adorable in her staple outfit. She is wearing a full-length light gray and white cotton dress with slits on either side and a full-length apron to cover it. Her 4C curl pattern coily hair is soft and fine, gray with white streaks. She wears it in pigtails braided on either side. Later in life, as I came to learn when I visited Ghana, this style is very popular among young Ghanaian girls. I discovered that hair braiding is an African cultural tradition that was practiced in our family.

We approach the driveway and Grandma Lene leaps out of her chair and hurriedly walks down the porch steps to greet us. Almost tripping over her skirt, she lifts up the bottom of her dress and, with a gleeful spirit, shouts, "Hey, y'all!" Her delicate mannerisms are unforgettable. She kisses me on the cheek and presses her face against mine. I feel her warm soft skin.

When reflecting on these childhood moments, I often associate the "Big House" with love and warmth. The "Big House" for many Black families represents the idea of domesticity and family, as it did during slavery for the white plantation owner and, in some cases, for the enslaved domestic servant. Grandma would be in the kitchen, cooking, and whites would come to the "Big House" for dinner. In *Black Aristocrats: Domestic Servants on the Antebellum Plantation*, Harper (1985) highlighted,

> Close associations that developed genuine affection of Whites toward Blacks also tended to develop ties of affection and respect that were reciprocated. It was not unusual for domestic servants to "consider themselves as forming part" of the master's family.

(p. 130)

Each summer when I travel to Virginia, the first stop is the "Big House." Despite the time gaps, nothing seems to change. All of the children, grandchildren, great-grandchildren, and nieces and nephews gather there for family time. Here Grandma Lene is, with those little slanted eyes. Now I know that it is from her that I get the shape of my eyes. Her bright smile fills the room with so much love and affection.

Everyone enters the "Big House" from the porch through the kitchen door, which is the main entrance. I am greeted with the scent that never seems to dissipate. For some reason, the smell is much more distinct this time. Maybe it's because I'm looking for it. The "Big House" has an aroma that I cannot seem to describe nor forget. It reminds me of the scent of old wood and tobacco. I say to myself, "What is that smell? Is it Grandma Lene's cooking?" Even at this young age, I am beginning to learn the history behind the legacy of the "Big House." For example, in 1938, my great-grandparents moved into the "Big House" when they were first married.

I wait for Grandma Lene to stop washing the dishes and lie down on the living room couch. I wait for her to tell me where to place my overnight bag. I have an upset stomach that is making me feel queasy and light headed. I am anxious to lie down. Grandma Lene guides me to her bedroom down the hall on the left, heading toward the rear of the house. There a huge wooden dresser stands in the hallway. I enter the bedroom and see a canopy bed that would take a ladder to climb up into. (Actually, there is a footstool in front of it for just that purpose.) Seeing its huge headboard and fluffy pillows, I am enticed to lie down. Trying to climb up into the bed is a difficult task. My legs have not grown quite long enough to manage the height of a Victorian bed with lots of blankets and feathered pillows. I lie down on the bed, praying that my belly ache subsides. Grandma Lene says, "Honey, tay' ya' a lil' rest and then y'all should soon feel betta." She reaches for a bottle of castor oil on the dresser. I watch her fill the spoon. She serves me two teaspoons of castor oil, which she says is good for stomach aches. Plantation owners and "overseers" used medicines and remedies to treat or prevent illness in both whites and the enslaved, such as calomel or castor oil, vinegar, and pine resin pills (Covey, 2007, p. 35).

Grandma turns off the light. I take a nap in the hope of feeling better when I awake. Three hours go by, and I awake from my nap. Grandma Lene comes in to check on me. I tell her that I am feeling much better. The "Big House" has a certain healing power about it.

When I get up, my hair is matted on one side. I walk over to the mirror to check my hair. Grandma Lene calls from the kitchen, "Deatra, you feelin' betta, honey?" Deatra is the name that my family calls me; because of their Southern accent, they cannot correctly pronounce my name. I gather myself and walk into the kitchen. I feel so much better. My headache is gone. My neck is no longer sore. My stomach is settled.

I enter the doorway between the kitchen and the living room, and I see my uncle, holding a dead squirrel upside down. He holds it over the sink as blood drips from its mouth; the squirrel is in one hand and a rifle in the other. The men in the family bring prey to the "Big House" for Grandma Lene to cook. He looks at me and laughs. I guess he sees the look on my face. This is the first time that I have seen a dead squirrel.

Grandma Lene is excited that food is here! My uncle hands her the squirrel and she places it on the countertop. She picks up her knife and skins it like a grape. She washes it with a scrub brush to be sure all hair is removed.

The "Big House" kitchen is something out of the colonial period, with a huge farm sink and a deep basin. The silver faucet knobs look like Christmas tree balls. Grandma Lene runs a heavy stream of water over the squirrel. She fills the sink with water and drops it into the sink to soak. Its little paws move. She squirts the hose to clean the dripping blood from its mouth. Then she makes a long incision across its back and splits the skin in half. Oh my goodness! The little claws are curled up like toenails. She proceeds to chop off its head and cuts it up into pieces as she would a chicken.

At the other end of the kitchen counter is a huge old-fashioned wood stove. She grabs one of the black cast iron frying pans from the cabinet and places it on the stove top. Grandma Lene used cooking tools similar to those of the enslaved. Covey and Eisnach (2009) highlighted comments made by Gibbs et al. (1980) on cooking tools that the enslaved used in the "Big House," noting "fireplaces, frying pans, skewers, cast iron pots, knives, and possibly pails, tea kettles, and Dutch ovens" (p. 60). The wood is burning and the stove is very hot. She pours the frying grease into the cast iron pan. The grease starts to pop from the heat. While the grease is heating, she is cutting the squirrel into pieces. The body of the squirrel is like a chicken breast. Grandma Lene makes a concoction of flour, egg, and milk, adds a little salt and pepper, and mixes it to make a batter for frying the squirrel. As on Southern plantations, squirrel was one of her favorite meats to prepare for the family.

Squirrel was one of the most common wild game meats for early white settlers and found its way into many stews (Taylor, 1982). Archeologists have found squirrel remains near slave quarters (Samford, 1996). Squirrel was tough and had to be cooked thoroughly, which may have led to cooks using it in stews. Genovese (1974) noted that squirrel pie served with dumplings was considered a delicacy among slaves.

(Covey, 2007, as cited in Covey and Eisnach, 2009, p. 124)

Hot grease is popping everywhere; it burns my cheek. Grandma Lene immediately puts butter on my face. Like the slave culture of enslaved Africans, my great-grandmother relies on home remedies to heal pain. According to Handler (2000): "Although White medical practitioners were occasionally hired, slaves overwhelmingly relied on self-help and depended on the resources of their own communities; as the years progressed, slaves continued to rely primarily on self-help" (p. 58). Grandma Lene applies what she calls "hog grease" to my face to relieve the burning sensation. Immediately, it feels better. This an old remedy that enslaved Africans used to soothe burns for their masters. An enslaved woman named Aunt Clara Walker said in an interview at the age of 111 that she recalled using "hog grease" to treat burns.

Dey killed a hog—fresh killed a hog. And de fry up de fat-fry it up wid some of de hog hairs an de'greased me good. An' it took all de fire out of de burns. Dey kept me greased for a long time.

(Covey, 2007, p. 135)

She flips the squirrel pieces into the frying pan so that they will brown evenly. The grease popping subsides and the aroma grows strong, much like that of fried chicken. She places a piece on a plate, cuts it into smaller pieces, and offers me a taste. I take a leap of faith and place it in my mouth. Already with a squirmy face, my mindset is to reject it. However, my heart won't allow me to reject such an offer. Game, animals, and hunting were all cultural traditions of the enslaved on the Southern plantation (Holloway, 2005). Grandma Lene is tickled pink at my positive reaction. The "Big House" is a place for celebrated family time and cherished moments with my elders. Elders are revered in the slave community. My family was no different.

3
Tobacco field

In this chapter we learn about the development of the tobacco industry in the Virginia colony.

Learning objectives

- To enhance awareness of how tobacco contributed to the growth and expansion of the Virginia British colonies.
- To learn the history of Africans as the chosen labor force in the British colonies.
- To explore customs in tobacco farming.
- To learn about tobacco farming as a cultural custom in the author's family heritage.

In 1899, my great-great-grandfather cultivated his own tobacco plantation in southern Virginia. Despite the horrors behind the history of its inception, the colonial Chesapeake tobacco trade left a legacy of four generations of Black farmers in my family. During the colonial period, owing to the labor of enslaved Africans and some white indentured servants, tobacco became the most profitable cash crop in the English colonies of Virginia, Maryland, and other colonies in the upper northern regions of the South (Main, 2014). The Tidewater region of eastern Virginia, which includes Maryland and Virginia, is the prime location for the tobacco industry. This area later developed into a massive economic empire along the Chesapeake Bay, which is approximately 200 miles long and 20 miles wide and comprises docks, waterways, and expanded terrain that is prime for the tobacco trade (Kulikoff, 2012; Main, 2014; Northup, 1970).

As the largest colony in the Americas during this period, Virginia relied heavily on the tobacco trade for financial security. British colonist John Rolfe of Jamestown, Virginia, foresaw the tobacco industry as the most promising means of economic expansion in the new colonies (Northrup, 1970). Virginia was also the most populous of the initial 13 colonies, and Maryland had a higher population than New York (Price, 1964). Over time, both colonies benefited from their resources.

Initially, the Virginia Company, founded in 1607, struggled to secure financial stability in the tobacco industry. Labor shortages became a major issue that affected profits to sustain operations. White indentured servants contracted to work only 5 to 10 years to earn their keep to remain in the Americas or to return to their homeland. These short-term labor contracts created a high turnover and an inconsistent labor force, leading to low tobacco production (Alderman, 1975). On occasion, the time commitment tended to be longer if the female indentured laborer was a pregnant woman during the term of servitude.

The first 20 Africans who arrived in Jamestown in 1619 began their oppression in the New World through the system of indentured servitude. However, owing to cultural, physical, and language differences from the British colonists, their legal status was not yet clearly defined. European colonists made attempts to enslave Native Americans; however, battles over land, malnutrition, and high death and disease rates among the colonists compromised their ability to enforce control over the native population (Herbert, 1970). In the first 30 years of colonial settlement (1607 to 1637) in Virginia and Maryland, the foundation of the exploitation of Africans as enslaved people in the tobacco industry was established and secured (Kulikoff, 2012). The tobacco industry started to flourish and the Virginia tobacco empire was born. Few white indentured servants were relied on in this period. According to Price (1956):

> We do know that "An Inventory of the Estate of Nathaniel Harrison Esquire, Decd." dated July 15, 1728, included a "Cutting House" containing a "Tob[acco] Engine," screws, cutting knives, etc., and an "Old Chest with old cutt tob[acco]." The meagerness of the equipment (e.g., three cutting knives) is inconsistent with manufacture on a commercial scale but quite consistent with the internal needs of an establishment containing 56 Negro slaves "At the Home-house" and 100 elsewhere plus three indentured white servants and one free mulatto servant.
>
> (p. 4)

England, which ruled the New World until the American Revolution of 1776, developed an interest in the importation of tobacco from the colonies (Clemens, 1975). Tobacco became the prime cash crop import from the Chesapeake Bay to Britain.

> In the second and third quarters of the eighteenth-century, however, there was a marked resumption of growth reaching in round numbers about 50 million pounds' weight in 1738–1742, 70 million in 1752–1756, and 100 million in 1771–1775. This last was more than

three times the level at the turn of the century or in the mid-1720s.

(Price, 1956, p. 497)

In the late seventeenth century, the focus on securing a labor force for the mass production of tobacco turned to Black Africans.

Childhood memory

One would think that growing up in the North would create a social distance in me from the southern "field." For southern Black farmers, the field referred to connectedness to energy, cultivation, growth, and prosperity, and this connection never faded. The "Big House" and the family tobacco plantation that surrounded it were my field and have contributed to my cultural and racial identity as an African American.

My mother was raised on our family tobacco plantation. She often shared stories with me of what it was like for her as a child growing up in the "tobacco field" or in the "country." These beloved stories have always made me feel proud to be a descendant of enslaved Africans and modern-day Black farmers from the American South. My mother described to me one summer as a teenager when she worked with my great-grandfather in the tobacco field. She rode on the back of great-grandpa's pickup truck, the sweat dripping from her face in the hot sun beating down on her head, and the mosquitoes eating her alive.

Every time my mother opens her box of family treasure stories, I am drawn closer to our enslaved ancestors who established plantation life in the slave community.

The work involved in growing tobacco is complicated; it is explored later in this book. It was one of the main sources of income for my family for generations. Great-grandpa was revered in his community, not only as the largest Black employer, but as a very giving and supportive man and a tough negotiator. Being the pillar of his community, great-grandpa hired out field hands to plant, grow, and pick tobacco to sell at the market for profit. He built a small house on the "Big House" property for the workers.

The workers were like a part of the family. They traveled from far distances just to work in the tobacco field for him. Providing housing alleviated the hardship of traveling long distances to the field. The field hands stayed during the week and went home on weekends. This practice was common among planters who could afford to house their employees on the "Big House" property. Grandma Lene cooked for the men and washed their clothes and tended to her eight children. She prepared fresh vegetables from the "Big House" garden and meats that were cured on the property. Through my personal experience and her storytelling, I am able to capture the day-to-day experiences in the life of a country girl on a tobacco plantation.

A gift given to my great-grandpa from his rumored father, a white plantation owner who lived only miles up the road, was 500 acres of tobacco spread across the community. Great-grandpa passed in 1966.

By the time I came along, my twin great-uncles were the sole owners and operators of the tobacco field that had been left by my great-grandpa.

My memories of the field begin at about the age of seven. Throughout my lifetime, I have known my twin great-uncles to wear the same loose-fitting uniform overalls, baseball cap, and work boots every day—even on Sundays, which for Black Southerners is the Lord's day, the day of rest. The enslaved Africans were required to wear "work" clothes or uniforms on the plantation. "Garments doled out to slaves throughout the American colonies tended to be drab, uniform and limited to relatively few items" (White and White, 1995a, p. 154). I believe that my twin great-uncles adopted many of their farming customs from their grandfather, my great-great-grandfather who was born in 1856.

Technology gradually became a part of my family's agricultural and farming management. However, for the majority of our family history, manual planting, growing, and picking of tobacco were practiced customarily. Until the Industrial Revolution, plantation machinery was scarce. From that time forward, machinery took away the need for much manual labor in agricultural and tobacco farming.

Although I feel the pain of that legacy because of what my ancestors endured, I know that, without the African cultural survival started on the Southern plantation, my family heritage would be quite different.

The smell of tobacco permeates the air. As a child, I sometimes feel out of place when going down South to visit family. I am a "city girl" for the most part, born and raised in the North. However, owing to living my life as the daughter of a true "Southern belle" in a household immersed in Southern traditions, I've grown accustomed to my family culture and ways of knowing. We raise flue-cured or bright lightweight tobacco. The tobacco leaves are harvested in the summer, usually beginning the process in late July or August. Walking down the long roads pulling tobacco leaves off the plant, depending on the height of the stalks, could require three trips back and forth, picking and piling the leaves. We watched my great-uncles harvest the leaves. The only way to describe the tobacco itself is that it is light, bright, and flue cured at harvest time. A little town called Brookneal houses a tobacco market. My great-uncles take the tobacco to the market and auction off the plants. There are lots of people there to sell their tobacco plants on what is known as Tobacco Lane. There are two types of tobacco: flue-cured and smoke-cured. We raised flue-cured tobacco, which is used for cigarettes, cigars, and snuff. On the plantation, we have horses and mules that we use to haul the tobacco after curing drying it. All of the land that was passed on to my great-grandpa serves as the lifeline to our family farming business.

My twin great-uncles learned as young children everything there was to know about tobacco field. They were pulled out of school in the sixth grade at the age of 12 to raise tobacco and work the field. They knew how to pick and process the tobacco. For many Black families in the South during the Jim Crow era, it was commonplace for younger siblings to be pulled out of school to help on the plantation.

My cousin and I exchanged memories of the tobacco-picking process that took place around the late 1970s. My great-uncles worked from sun up to sun down, six days a week, with one day off a week: Sundays, for church. They rose at 5:00 a.m. and returned home at sundown. Back then, the tobacco was picked and tied manually. Horses and carts were used to transport the loads. There was no irrigation system. My cousins can recall when they had to run water through the hose to fill the containers and then manually irrigate acres of land. Gender roles were integral to the operation. The men were assigned to run the water and put it in the large containers. They pumped the water out of a trailer that was hitched to the back of a truck. The summer weather, in the middle of tobacco season, was always hot. By noon, it was 100 degrees in the shade. They would pick tobacco for four or five hours in the morning and then transport a load on the trailer back to the barn. The trailers were attached to the plant in order to pull the tobacco. My great-uncles would drive the machine out into the field and the tobacco pickers would place the plant on the back of the trailers. To tie the tobacco, the men would hold it in a stationary position and the children or other helpers would hold the tobacco together in bunches. Men or women would tie each bundle. The men would use sticks to hang the tobacco in the barn. They would climb up on the beams in the barn and pass the tobacco in an assembly line. Then they would hang the leaves across the beams. This was approximately a three-day process. There was no electricity in the barn, so my great-uncles lit lanterns and checked on the bundles throughout the night. This process was performed completely by hand.

Over time, my family purchased an automated machine to tie the tobacco. This reduced the labor by three or four steps. The kids were responsible for removing the tobacco from the trailers. The women placed the tobacco on a conveyor belt. It looked like an oversized needle that tied the tobacco. They would lay it down on a stick, one layer at a time. The machine tied the plant.

Then they would remove it from the stick and pass it to the first worker on the assembly line and then to three or four laborers.

When hanging tobacco, they had to make sure that the temperature in the room was right. The women made sure that the tobacco cured properly. They would remove it from the stick to make sure that it was securely tied. Once it was cured, they wrapped it to hold the cluster of leaves together. Stringing tobacco manually was extremely difficult but, over time, it became standardized. By the 1980s, my great-uncles had purchased our first tractor, a John Deere. We no longer had to use a horse and cart to haul the tobacco.

The cluster of stalks weighed up to 200 pounds each. The children would walk it down to the truck so that my great-uncles could prepare it for transporting to the market for auction. The heavier the stalks, the better. The men would place them on the back of a large truck. We would auction off 25,000 to 30,000 pounds of tobacco at a time.

This is a story of community support. Stacking tobacco was a group effort. Despite the horrific events of slavery, most labor practices were done through group effort. The tobacco fields of the modern era operate similarly.

Another similarity with slavery is that farmers negotiated for the highest price. One could earn up to $100,000 for the sale of tobacco at an auction. However, mad cow disease and Philip Morris lawsuits against tobacco farmers and manufacturers in the 1980s stunted the growth of the industry. In addition, tariffs on tobacco increased and production of the plant decreased, which drove farmers out of business. This is a message of family, unity, group work, labor, and production. Work ethic and pride were the driving forces behind our family farming business. The skills and techniques of tobacco farming are the legacy of my enslaved African ancestors.

As a child, tobacco picking seemed like a game to me. My cousin and I learned to drive a tractor at the age of 13. My great-uncle said that he taught us so that we would be prepared to drive a car when we reached the age. I always thought that he was preparing us to work the field one day!

The best part of the workday was the aroma of Grandma Lene's cooking coming from the kitchen window. While the workers were out on in the tobacco field, Grandma Lene was in the kitchen preparing their meals: string beans, collard greens, and cabbage seedlings from her garden.

I try to imagine having to work the fields in the dreadful heat, as my ancestors did. How the South must have hurt with pain and misery! I look up and see a rainbow, wondering where the end of it leads.

4
Farming and gardening

In this chapter we learn about horticultural traditions and farming practices in Africa and in the American South.

Learning objectives

- To learn the history of "slave gardens" on the Southern plantation.
- To explore the farming practices in the Northern Region of Ghana.
- To examine slave foods in common with African American food traditions.
- To learn common Southern recipes and Southern home remedies used by African Americans and enslaved Africans.
- To learn about farming and gardening as a cultural custom in the author's family heritage.

Rich horticultural traditions such as gardening, farming, and bartering homegrown foods reflect my family's ancestral connection to the continent of Africa. Great-Grandma Lene, Grandmother Cathy, and paternal Grandmother Nana unwittingly lived their lives steeped in the agriculture customs and mores passed on by my enslaved ancestors. These influential women in my life were brilliant in their horticultural knowledge to raise their own produce for family and community sustenance. This knowledge was integral to the development of African societies. There is a broad lack of appreciation for the indigenous farming practices on the African continent that were transported through the transatlantic slave trade to the Southern plantation. Many of those who were enslaved from various parts of Africa contributed to Western food culture (Sousa and Raizada, 2020). Our ancestors must be acknowledged for their contributions to horticulture in Northern America portrayed as invaluable to people of African descent and American culture.

On the Southern plantation, enslaved Africans developed slave gardens (better known in the antebellum period as slave "patches") to grow fruits and vegetables to supplement the inadequate food supply provided by the slaveholder (Westmacott, 1992), similar to farming practices in West Africa.

Slave gardens were a form of independence on the Southern plantation. According to Eisnach and Covey (2019), "Slave gardens, or 'patches,' were typically located near the slave cabins, or even occasionally, in the most remote brambled boundaries of the plantation where clearing had never been done" (p. 11). To give the enslaved a sense of "ownership," slave gardens were generally placed near the slave residence, away from the main house, or in forests and under-brushed areas.

Farming practices in the Northern Region of Ghana

While in Ghana, I did research on Ghanaian farmers and interviewed West Africans who were willing to share their experiences about African crop domestication in the Northern Region of Ghana. Africans come from primarily agrarian societies, like those of the American South. Based on my research, many of the crop migration histories out of Africa to areas throughout the African diaspora contributed to the household foods, nutrition, and cultures of the enslaved Africans in the New World. The value that African families placed on farming is similar to the values of my family in Virginia and of the enslaved who were allowed to have slave gardens on the Southern plantation. Growing one's own crops is pivotal to the nutrition and health of the Ghanian people, as it is in my family heritage. Farming in Ghana is central to the lives of the Ghanaian people, as it is in my family.

Mohammed Nurudeen Musah grew up in the Northern Region of Ghana and farmed there as a child. He shared his life experiences and knowledge about Ghanaian agricultural practices in the Northern Region of Ghana. In turn, I shared with him my familial farming and gardening practices in Virginia.

Question 1
Please tell me your knowledge of farming in Ghana.

> Farming among the African descendance [sic] runs deep with "rooted ties." The [farming] people own farms or the families own the farm and they do their

own work there. At the end of the harvest, the family uses it when it is finished and they have to find other alternatives to boost whatever is left over. They grow some of the best crops and keep the seeds for the next harvest.

Question 2

What types of crops are predominately grown in Ghana?

The types of crops that they grow are usually corn, maize, millet, peanuts (Ghanaian), soya beans, and green leafy vegetables.

Question 3

Please tell me more about the farming practices in Ghana.

Those who live close to the valleys do rice farming, and mango farming, and shea butter. Most of the shea butter is grown up north. They are not in the southern parts of Ghana. They are usually up north. People do not cultivate the nuts like farms do it. They are usually wild trees. The seeds are seasonal. The women pick them and go through the normal process of trying to prepare them, save them and use them to make the shea butter later or sell them to those who are buying them. This is usually the process. What they have done to the shea butter is that the tree is very good for fire wood. So, people were cutting it down but in most communities up north it is illegal to cut down a shea butter tree. So, they do not cut them down in modern times. Also, the natives try to control wild fires. When people go hunting they would use fires to drive the wild animals out. However, in most parts of the northern sector people are asked not to practice this tradition.

Question 4
How many regions are there in the Northern Region of Ghana? In which region is the shea butter grown?

There are now three regions in Ghana: northern, western, and eastern. These are currently the major regions that were in the northern sector. These are the places where you find the shea butter tree.

Question 5
How else would you describe the farming process in the Northern Region?

There are people who go around and work on other people's farms and they get paid for it. They do not have their own farms. This applies largely to the Ghanaian families from the northern sector of Ghana. Usually if we have people coming from outside they are usually people from international agencies such as NGO who are trying to assist. But normally they work for themselves or work on somebody else's farm. Also, people work on other family farms. Most people do not get paid for their farm work as it is a family arrangement. The pay that they get is the food from the farming season. And when the family has a need then they will sell some of the products to cover the cost. For example, if someone is going to have a family wedding, they would sell some of the products to cover the cost of the wedding, because it is collective produce. When individuals own farms, they get the harvest for themselves only. However, there are some groups and organizations that invest for someone who may not be able to afford 5 or 10 acres of land. If I go to the organization and do the plowing then they will give me seeds and I will plant them. Then afterwards, I will pay them back with produce. The leftovers are given to the farm owner. This is the system for cotton. The farmers plant cotton seeds just like other crops. The farmers plow and fertilize the plants then return to harvest them and share them with the state agency. The agency buys the crops at cost plus interest and distributes any leftovers to the farmers who did the labor. The same process takes place with the corn and soya beans in some parts of the Northern Region. But for those who have the means and do their own farming, they cover their own expenses and keep whatever belongs to them. They do not have to share it with anyone.

Government involvement is strong in the political structure in Ghana. One thing that Kwame Nkrumah, former president of Ghana, did for this country was to unite it. We are a very diverse group in Ghana. Ghana has 80 distinct ethnic groups. Over 350 official dialects and 150 languages. But Ghanaians recognized that they are Ghanaian. Despite whatever corruption that may exists in this country, everyone is proud to be a Ghanaian. Nobody tries to hide their pride. President Nkrumah helped to bridge the gap. In the northern sector the Ashanti people are seen as backward people. Even in the language of the Ashanti people. Sometimes you will hear it. It is like these people are from the bush. The northern sector of the country.

Question 6
What does "bush people" mean? Does it mean that they are uneducated?

Yes, they are from the villages and such. Similar to the perception we have of southerner farmers. Uneducated, and village … but they have a very constructed political system that dates as far back as pre-colonial times. So, they are not as backwards as they might be perceived to be. The problem is that part of Ghana is rainy, or wet season. We have only two seasons: a dry season and a wet season. We have rainy season when it rains all of the time and a dry season when it barely rains. In the southern part, which is around the coast, we have longer wet seasons. In the northern sector we have shorter wet seasons which means that those up north can only farm once a season. So, if they don't get their plants right, if they don't do their farming correctly everything falls apart. However, the southern sector which has the rain forest and as we go through Kumasi, and all of the places that we visited, you can see the greenery. It is usually very harsh up there even though it does not rain as much as it should. You can still see the greenery because the weather is different from the northern sector. After the harvest, they have to sometimes remain there for seven or eight months before the next rain comes. And because the natives need to work and find something to sustain themselves, some natives move down to the city of Kumasi or Accra to seek employment opportunities. For some of the children this is another push factor that brings them to the streets because there are no opportunities up there for them. In some parts of the north there is no electricity.

In some parts of the northern sector the people prefer to be in the urban areas. Accra and Kumasi are the two major cities that we have, so everyone want to live in the city.

Question 7

Are these people skilled in the types of jobs that are offered in Accra and Kumasi? What are the jobs that they come to do?

They are very skilled. Dr. Ali, one of the professors at the University, is from the northern sector. He has a traditional name. Muslims live mostly in the southern extract.

My interview with Nurudeen on the agrarian practices of Ghanaian people aided in understanding the connection of my family's farming practices with those on the continent of Africa. The value that is placed on farming in the Ghanaian community is equal to that of my family. Farming, bartering, and community support are traditional in Africa and a large part of my Southern roots.

Westmacott (1992) supported this history by highlighting comments by others on a common agrarian foundation between African farming and the Southern plantation. His analysis supports the idea that enslaved Africans were once transported directly from African agrarian societies to the Southern plantation in the New World. This transported farming and gardening practices to the slaveholders' estates. Westmacott (1992) noted:

> Africans were able to adapt to plantation life because they came from agrarian tribes. There are common traditions among agrarian peoples, and probably the slaves were able to invest some of those of the plantation owners with their own meanings quite rapidly. After the Congressional ban on slave importation in 1808, most slaves were smuggled into America directly from Africa rather than through the West Indies.
>
> (p. 16)

Not all enslaved persons were permitted to have gardens: the men and women in bondage who were given permission to raise their own gardens for supplemental dietary and nutritional needs were fortunate. Although the slave owners set forth strict and harsh rules to maintain control of the plantation, the gardens that they permitted people to cultivate afforded the slaves some autonomy and liberation from oppressed conditions (Fett, 2002).

My grandmothers shared their Southern way of life by passing on their agricultural knowledge to our family from generation to generation, providing prosperity and cultural richness to our family lineage.

Childhood memory

I can almost hear the sound of morning dew accumulating around the flowers outside Cathy's front stoop. Grandmother Cathy is referenced as just "Cathy" in this book. Cathy is not her actual name. I gave her this name after my baby doll, "Chatty Cathy," when I was five years old.

Early in the morning, a rooster crowed. A truck passed by. The puppy across the road barked incessantly. The crickets chirped. The sounds of country life were welcoming to my ears. The sun rose and set beyond the pasture.

Cathy had an apple tree in her backyard. Most of the time, we did not have to pick the apples directly off the tree; when they were ripe enough, they dropped to the ground.

In Virginia, the apple season is in August, when most of the apples fall to the ground like leaves from a tree. Cathy and I collected apples from the grass; if they remained there too long, raccoons, deer, and groundhogs would devour them. One Saturday morning, Cathy asked me to collect about 10 apples so she could make fried apples for breakfast. This was her recipe:

- To feed up to 4 to 6 people, gather 10 to 12 apples
- Wash the apples thoroughly
- Peel the skin off
- Slice into 4 thin pieces
- Heat ½ tablespoon of butter or olive oil in a frying pan until hot

- Add any amount of brown or white sugar as according to taste preference
- Place sliced apples in frying pan
- Sprinkle sugar evenly over apple slices
- Cover frying pan with top for about 5 minutes
- Remove pot top to prevent apples from getting too mushy
- Flip them as they cook until they are golden brown.

Cathy also made apple pie and candy apples with apples from her tree.

It was 6:00 a.m. on Sunday morning. I heard Cathy getting dressed in the next room. Every morning, she rose at the crack of dawn to do her horticultural activities. Early rising to do the farming and gardening was a requirement of the slaveholder. According to Eisnach and Covey (2019), "The men and women who tended them [gardens] had to do it at the beginning or end of fifteen- to sixteen-hour work days or on Sundays" (p. 11). I peeked around the corner and saw her getting dressed. She put on her girdle and torn pantyhose, pink and white smock, wide-legged loose-fitting pink and white pants, and leather closed-toe shoes with the sole coming unglued. This was her staple gardening uniform. There is an image in one of our family photo albums that is more than 60 years old of her standing in the middle of the garden holding a flowerpot with her rhands on her hips.

As I watched from around the corner, she grabbed her flowerpot and filled it with water. I got dressed and went outside to inquire as to whether she needed help. The storm door slammed behind me from the wind. I saw the beautiful flowers that had bloomed almost overnight. As I walked across the thick green grass to reach her, I saw what appeared to be a colony of wasps flying toward me. I almost froze but I knew that I had to get away, so I ran inside my Uncle Joe's trailer, located next door to Cathy's house. Down South, the bees are like a part of the family. Every summer, they welcomed me home. Unfortunately, Cathy was not as fortunate. A wasp flew up her pants leg as she tried to run into the house. I had noticed earlier that day that there was a wasp's nest in the corner under the car porch. However, it appeared to be harmless. I ran out of the trailer over to my grandmother to ensure that she was okay. Cathy hastily asked me to grab the pack of Camel cigarettes on the kitchen counter in Uncle Joe's trailer. Bewildered, I asked her why she needed his cigarettes. She didn't answer, as the pain from the sting had her full attention. I followed her instructions and gave her the pack of cigarettes. She took out one cigarette, cracked it open, and extracted the tobacco. She then rubbed it on her right leg, directly over the pain. Once the pain appeared to subside, she responded to my inquiry and shared with me that tobacco is used for bee stings. Covey (2007, p. 114), in his book *African American Slave Medicine*, highlighted Fleming's findings that some Native Americans used tobacco to treat toothaches, mosquito bites, and bee stings.

Although she was born in 1921, 56 years after Emancipation, my grandmother embodied slave culture in her daily life. Unfortunately, she did not have any formal education on the enslavement of Africans.

Like most African Americans born during slavery, Reconstruction, or the Jim Crow era, Black history was not taught in classrooms. What limited information our families obtained was shared through the traditional practice of generational storytelling, passing along family history from one generation to the next. My grandmother had only a fourth- or fifth-grade education. Aside from storytelling or her own life experiences, she did not learn anything about slavery, Reconstruction, or Jim Crow in school. She inherited most of her cultural traditions from her father (my great-grandfather), as her mother had passed away when Cathy was a teenager, and her older siblings.

Gardening as an integral part of our family life, as in northern Ghana, represents freedom, independence, healthful living, and tradition. Cathy always referred to her garden of turnip greens as a "patch." These green leafy plants were confined to a small space in the corner of her garden. As in Africa, her garden contained cowpeas or black-eyed peas, tomatoes, cucumbers, string beans, sweet potatoes, white potatoes, okra, and leafy turnip greens, all of which flourished like a forest of vegetables.

Cathy preserved and stored vegetables and fruits in glass jars every year. Instead of glass jars, enslaved people stored fruits and vegetables in tin cans and sealed them with wax. Covey and Eisnach (2009, p. 77) noted Susan Smith's comments on how enslaved people stored fruits and vegetables: "Some food was canned in tin cans and sealed with canning wax. Preserves were made of the fruit." Canning was an economic measure to manage family finances. Luckily, Cathy was able to reuse the same jars, but the metal tops had to be replaced. She cooked the preserved vegetables and fruits such as apples and peaches in a large pressure cooker, then stored them in jars for the winter. She made her own jelly from the fruits grown in the garden. Grandma Lene used to preserve sweet potatoes and white potatoes in big sacks and stored them in the "Big House" basement, where it was cool. This practice is similar to that used by the enslaved. "Slaves used root cellars year round to store foods" (Covey and Eisnach, 2009, p. 952).

Cathy had so much left over from year to year that we were not able to eat all of it. The preserves lasted for years. To keep track of storage freshness, she wrote the date on the top of the jar.

To keep the garden and yard manicured, Cathy cut her own grass once a week, using a riding mower. Her garden remained pristine. Managing it took dedication and persistence. I was in awe at the delicate nature of her management.

Cathy lived to be 98 years old. I know that this longevity can be attributed to her diet. She ate only healthful homegrown foods or items that she purchased from the health food store. In essence, food production had become the cultural capital of the enslaved in the South. Eisnach and Covey (2019) wrote, "In spite of the many restrictions and oppression imposed by slavery, gardening, nevertheless, was a widespread pursuit for the enslaved throughout the South" (p. 11).

My grandmothers were born into the life of farming and gardening, one generation removed from American slavery. The tenacity that built the South emerged from the backs of the enslaved Africans.

Buttermilk

Some stories that I heard as a child, before I was old enough to go out into the fields, claimed that my Grandma Lene made everything from "scratch." At the time, I did not know what this meant. Grandma Lene had a garden full of vegetables and chickens. She made her own buttermilk from fresh cow's milk. Buttermilk was fed to enslaved Africans on the Southern plantation because "Southern planters advised that slaves should not have sweet milk but only soured milk or buttermilk" (Moor, 1989, as cited in Covey and Eisnach, 2009, p. 138).

Dipping cornbread in buttermilk was a common practice in my family. For Thanksgiving dinner, Grandma Lene set the table with cornbread, gravy, rice, turkey, and all the trimmings. She put buttermilk in a small soup bowl and placed it in the center of the table. According to Covey and Eisnach (2009), enslaved Africans drank buttermilk and used it to sweeten their cornbread. "A typical meal for slaves was buttermilk poured over cornbread prepared by either themselves or their owners" (p. 139).

Grandma Lene had a way to make time for special things, such as preparing home-grown foods for the family. She knew that the family loved her home cooking and she prepared our meals with love.

Grandma Lene's recipe for making buttermilk is quite easy. My mother shared the recipe with me. She had fond memories of watching Grandma Lene make buttermilk. This storytelling was a bonding experience for my mother and me. Laughing and talking about the wonderful memories of her childhood in the South was inspiring. She shared the following recipe.

> You take the cow's milk and use a tablespoon of vinegar, as it starts to curl. It doesn't take a long time to curl. Then she would add a teaspoon of vinegar. Let it sit until it curls up. Buttermilk has a yellowish tint to it from the vinegar. After 10 minutes, the milk thickens.

When my mother shared this memory, I asked her whether buttermilk attracted flies, as in the folk song from the 1800s "Flies in the Buttermilk, Shoo Fly Shoo." She told me that buttermilk does attract flies like most churned foods; however, most people back then in the South did not pay attention to flies; they just tolerated them. Flies were a part of life.

Grandma Lene used buttermilk to make hoe cakes and buttermilk biscuits. The shape of the hoe cake is a bit odd: much like a crooked pancake. Grandma Lene's hoe cake recipe and biscuits include a combination of baking soda, flour, lard, and buttermilk.

I can envision the family farm in my mind—the horses, cows, pigs, slaughter house, cured hogs hanging in the barn, and the hen house full of chickens and baby chicks. Along with flower and vegetable gardening, my family also raised and cured their own meats and dairy products. This too was prevalent practice in the slave community of the antebellum South. Olmsted (1860, as cited in Westmacott, 1992, p. 16) wrote that "the slaves in Virginia were permitted to raise pigs and poultry, and in summer could always grow as many vegetables as they wanted". When I was spending summers in the South, we ate fresh chicken that was raised on our farm. This was a delicacy in my family.

Grandma would take the chicken and break its neck, then cut off its head. The chicken flew around wingless and eventually collapsed and died. Then she would defeather the chicken, cut it into small pieces, and boil it in a big pot of salt water. Grandma Lene was proud of her fresh chicken dishes. She cultivated other homemade products, as well. Like my maternal grandmother Cathy, she had a flourishing garden in which she grew string beans, corn, lima beans, beets, black-eyed peas, carrots, potatoes, and grapes.

She used the grapes to make "slo" wine, as she called it. My mother shared her memories of Grandma Lene making the wine in the yard of the "Big House." She made the wine in big barrels with a plunger, which has the same effect as walking on the grapes or churning and pressing them. Afterward, she let it ferment. Grandma Lene's homemade "slo" wine was a combination of red and white grapes from her personal vine.

Grandma Lene also made ice cream from scratch. It is a very simple process. She used fresh dairy milk drawn from the cows raised on our farm and brought to her by my twin great-uncles. She added sugar, salt and milk in a saucepan, which made a cream. She did not have the benefit of an electric mixer, so she stirred it herself until it reached the thickness that she wanted. Then she added vanilla bean and chilled it in the refrigerator. She let it freeze until it became solid enough to serve. Grandma Lene took pride in her ice cream making because she knew that it brought joy to the family. Grandma Lene's ice cream would always taste better the next day. The anticipation of waking up the next morning ready to be served Grandma Lene's ice cream special put a smile on my face. This made her happy to know that I loved her ice cream so much. She made sure to have enough when I came to visit.

She made homemade apple, peach, blueberry, and blackberry cobblers, too. Her blueberry cobblers were so sweet! Blueberries, sugar, and butter formed a mixture in a saucepan. She never could get the blue stains out of the saucepan. She made a thick sauce, then took the berries and sugar and mixed them on the stove and added more blueberries. She was careful not to overcook them or they would turn to mush. She mixed blueberries, sugar, and butter to make the syrup. Then she made her own crust with flour, sugar, milk, and baking powder. Her crusts always came out flaky. She was a great baker! Like the enslaved in the antebellum South, my grandmother used cast iron cooking pots and pans. Otto and Burns (1983), in their article "Black Folks and Poor Buckras: Archeological Evidence of Slave and Overseer Living Conditions on an Antebellum Plantation," mentioned that the slave cabin refuse contained only fragments of cast iron cooking pots and that they were essential to "slave cooking" in the slave quarters (Covey and Eisnach, 2009, p. 57).

We also raised pigs on our farm; from these, Grandma Lene made fresh chitterlings for the family. She boiled or fried them with flour and seasoning. My mother adopted the fried chitterling tradition. At the time, I thought that chitterlings were the best thing ever! Chitterlings came directly from the pigs on our farm. My twin great-uncles slaughtered the pig and cut it up in pieces. I remember the hog farmers who would prepare the pig. It was an art form to maximize what one could take from the animal to eat or sell. The enslaved slaughtered hogs in the early morning (Covey and Eisnach, 2009). This was a delicacy, prevalent among the enslaved in the South.

> Virtually nothing was wasted on the plantation, including the intestines of hogs. Pork, chitterlings, or chitlins, although associated with the African Americans and made from the small intestines of pigs, were consumed by all in the South.
>
> (Hilliard, 1972, as cited in Covey and Eisnach, 2009, p. 106)

As did the enslaved African on the Southern plantation, our family raised and preserved meats, such as chicken, pork, and beef. Some of my cousins who lived in separate homes built on the "Big House" estate did not know what a supermarket was until age eight! Our hog farmers had to know which internal organs were salvageable and safe to be preserved. This required folk and inherited knowledge. We are an amazing and brilliant people. Slave culture is indeed our legacy. This tradition was passed down from my great-grandma and great-grandpa's parents.

My great-uncles did what is called "aging" the pig meat. Beef did not take as long to "age" as did pork. The process to tenderize a carcass occurs more quickly. Cow skin is not that thick; pig skin is much thicker. Pigs are mostly made up of fat. Cows had to be aged for about four or five days before cutting. The temperature had to be below a certain level and my uncles were confident with the process. Too high a temperature spoils the meat. The cooling process had to be precise to keep the meat from spoiling. During the off season, when the barns on our farm were not used for tobacco, cows and pigs were stored there separately.

After the meat was cured, my great-uncles bartered or sold it to people in the community.

Our hog farmers wrapped the pig and cow meat in wax paper, packaged it, and stored it in the freezer. They had to make sure that it stayed tender prior to cooking. We also made our own bacon, pig's feet, ribs, and cow tongue. Smoked bacon is cured pig meat cooked on a low-heat fire. This is what gives it the smoky flavor. Cow meat is not smoked; it is cured. Pig bacon, pork ribs, and tails were stored in the freezer. We pasteurized meats and produce on our farm. We had to eat the meats quickly before they spoiled. After the meat thawed, which could take a long period of time, Grandma Lene seasoned it with all types of fresh spices, such as garlic, onion, cumin, ginger, and paprika, all grown in her garden. This tradition is a legacy of enslaved Africans on the Southern plantation.

> Whatever meat plantation owners made available to slaves usually of poor quality and quantity. This is one of the reasons why slaves added so many spices to their dishes. When the chops, hams, and loins went to the "Big House", typically slaves got the leftover ears, tails, feet, fat, ribs, tripe, chicken feet, heads, tongues and innards.
>
> (Cusick, 1995, and Yentsch, 2007, as cited in Covey and Eisnach, 2009, p. 97)

Our family often made pot roast with the beef and pork roast or ham from the pig.

Sweet potatoes and tomatoes

I grew up on sweet potatoes and tomatoes. Homemade sweet potato pies, sweet potato casserole, fried sweet potato, and baked sweet potato were made from the sweet potatoes grown in my grandmother's garden. In the South, we used sweet potatoes more as a dessert than as an entrée. My grandmothers made sweet mashed potatoes. The sweet potatoes grew on a vine like regular potatoes.

Our family farm had tomatoes, too. One summer, my family grew more than five acres of tomatoes. My cousins ate tomatoes all year for breakfast, lunch, and dinner. My aunt made tomato soup, tomato sandwiches, fried green tomatoes, tomato salads, and tomato pie. They gave away hundreds of tomatoes to the community.

Bartering was another family practice that was used in return for services. My Aunt Ella, the youngest daughter of Grandma Lene, shared a personal story of bartering in our family. She explained that, when a debt was owed in the community, instead of collecting money, people would barter food, clothing, or labor on our family farm in exchange for services. Westmacott (1992) found that "slaves grew produce to supplement their diets and to give them something to barter with or to give away in return for services" (p. 16). The tomatoes and other homegrown vegetables from our garden, as well as meats, were used to pay debts to people in the community. My aunt shared a story of how our family bartered, especially when my great-grandfather was still living. She said that Mr. Bounty, a neighbor who lived down the road from the "Big House," owed my great-grandfather money for a tool but was unable to pay for it. Instead, he offered fresh vegetables that his wife had grown in their garden. This practice was common in the antebellum South and was an example of how Black families offered community and family support through gardening and farming.

5
Bare feet

In this chapter we learn the meaning of bare feet during slavery and how the practice evolved in American society.

Learning objectives

- To broaden awareness of the historical meaning of bare feet.
- To facilitate discussion on the reader's personal experiences with bare feet.
- To gain understanding of bare feet as an American and African cultural custom.
- To learn about bare feet stereotypes in American society.
- To learn about bare feet as a cultural custom in the author's family heritage.

The sun was hot, but my feet remained cool. I must admit that it was a peculiar sensation. The environmental aesthetics were pleasing to my eyes. As I looked up into the trees, I could see a spiraled web, similar to a cotton ball. Upon further examination, I saw that it was a web of spinning caterpillars—cocoons and silken nests spun by eastern tent caterpillars and fall webworms. This was a sign that I was getting close to the "Big House"!

In honor of my African ancestors, I fervently embrace my bare feet. The barefoot enslaved African, who symbolized all that is inferior and subordinate to the European elite, embodies my childhood innocence, virtue, and purity. Bare feet were mandated in some slave colonies to reinforce the notion of subservience and docility. While the horseshoe was bestowed on the horse to protect its feet, nothing was granted to the enslaved. According to Forte (2015), "Colonial decrees sometimes mandated that slaves go barefoot" (para. 1). Nevertheless, the enslaved African managed to overcome these challenges. Many had no choice but to work and live without anything on their feet. Some worked barefoot in the fields in horrid conditions, but they managed to survive their abhorrent situation. The Huck Finn Freedom Center published a narrative of a former slave named Emma Knight, who described her personal pain as an enslaved person with bare feet.

> We didn't have hardly no clothes and most of de time dey was just rags. We went barefoot until it got real cold. Our feet would crack open from de cold and bleed.
>
> (Jim's Journey: The Huck Finn Freedom Center, 2022, para. 1)

The grit and resilience of my enslaved ancestors empower me to express my contemplations and thoughts on bare feet as I deem appropriate. If it were not for their sacrifices, I may not ever have truly understood the significance of this slave custom.

Historically, bare feet have had various societal connotations. Bare feet have been romanticized, criminalized, dismissed, and shunned. Primarily attributed to those who were labeled as savage or barbarian, bare feet provoked negative visual stereotypes.

Bare feet have been made to be emblematic of unsophistication, impoverishment, and degradation. Despite these mischaracterizations, bare feet have provided me fond memories of my childhood and, as I would later learn, aided some African ancestors in their escape from slavery.

During periods of rebellions, the enslaved traveled miles in the night with bare feet in search of glimpses of independence and liberation. I can envision the scene that Adrienne M. Israel (2018) described of the barefoot enslaved fugitive fleeing from bondage along the Underground Railroad. She wrote the following in her book, *Free Blacks, Quakers, and the Underground Railroad in Piedmont North Carolina,* on enslaved Africans fleeing from bondage:

> Its portrayals often depict barefoot runaways dressed in tattered rags, searching the night sky for the North Star, walking stealthily through dark forests, feeling tree trunks for north hanging moss or for nails hammered through bark or into fence posts, directing them to safety.
>
> (p. 2)

I imagine that my ancestors were sleeping in the wilderness in the harsh conditions of freezing cold rain and scorching hot sun, swimming through bodies of deep and shallow waters, treading over stones and other objects, observed by nature and wild animals in the forests. However tortuous their journey might have been, their bare feet bestowed on them the strength and endurance to carry on.

Childhood memory

I can recall, as a child, walking down the road to the "Big House" to meet my cousins for playtime. Crossing the tobacco fields, uncertain of which direction my bare feet would take me, I experienced exhilaration and anticipation. Some of the best activities that we played were played in our bare feet: duck goose, freeze, hula hoop, hide and go seek, and tag. We would also race on the grass in our bare feet so we could run faster. Some of my fondest memories in the South are of walking and playing barefoot along the side of the road, on the thick grass and ice-cold dirt. I recall running and jumping barefoot in the creek water with my naked toes sinking into the pebbled sand. This is just a glimpse of my childhood memories.

My bare feet did not mean that I could not afford shoes. We were not poor. However, my perception of bare feet was poverty and mediocrity—the stereotype reserved for barefoot colored girls like me. My bare feet did not mean a lack of progress or culture. To the contrary, bare feet represent advancement to a higher level of Black consciousness in knowing that I am the legacy of enslaved Africans on the Southern plantation. Bare feet are a cultural phenomenon of sorts that transcends race, ethnicity, gender, and class. Nevertheless, barefoot Black girls are often depicted negatively in many magazines and books.

While walking barefoot, I would pass dilapidated buildings or small cabins that emerged beyond the tobacco fields. I suspected that these structures were part of the terrain where my enslaved ancestors rested their tired aching bodies after a hard day's labor. I envisioned that my ancestors were running barefoot from tree trunk to tree trunk in search of air, so that they could exhale. I could smell the distinct odor of freshly grown tobacco. As I skipped along barefoot, I plucked baby dandelions and blew the feathery leaves toward the sky as the wind added to my amusement.

Walking barefoot gave me a sense of playfulness and recalled happy songs. As I skipped along, I sang "Let Me Be Your Angel," by Stacey Lattisaw, my childhood idol from the 1980s.

When I arrived at the "Big House," I could see my cousins standing near the chicken house, barefoot, waiting for me to play a game of hide and go seek. Quickly, I ran over to them. We played for most of the afternoon. Playing barefoot was a common pastime for us. After all, it was our family tradition.

My grandmother, affectionately known as Cathy, used to clean and mop the floor in her bare feet. She removed her shoes, grabbed the mop and bucket, and went to work. When she swished the mop back and forth, there was a certain swagger about her movement, as if she were swaying to the beat of her favorite gospel song. For most of my childhood, Cathy sang in the church choir; the songs were embedded in her mind and subconsciousness. She loved to sing one hymn in particular while doing her household chores: "Take Me Back." She sang that song all day while mopping and cleaning in her bare feet; it echoed throughout the house. "Take me back, take me back dear lord, to the place where I first believed you." She encouraged me to sing the hymn in a church pageant when I was about 11 years old. I was terrified, but I knew that, with her encouragement, I could do it.

The floors in the kitchen were ceramic tile, which required mopping at least once a week. Cathy made a homemade cleaning mix of dish detergent and warm water and a drop of ammonia. She never got her feet wet when mopping the floor. She had a certain technique that started from the corner of the room and then worked her way in a reverse motion. She was an expert at this task. One day, I asked her why she cleaned in her bare feet. She told me that it was a generational custom that was passed on from her mother and grandmother. Cathy's grandmother was born into slavery. Cathy told me that working barefoot was a tradition in our family that was derived from her grandmother's brutal experiences of working barefoot on the plantation. Cathy said that bare feet allowed her to "get to the grit and dirt mo' betta." She worked a "day's work" as a domestic, cleaning for a wealthy white family in the local town. When I was about 9 or 10 years old, I went with her to the housekeeping jobs and watched her clean the entire house in her bare feet.

Society has demonized bare feet in various ways. Signs in department stores and restaurants read "No Bare Feet." The perception is that bare feet are unkempt. However, bare feet are a family tradition deeply rooted in slavery.

During the Colonial era, shoes were a novelty, an emblem of status and wealth. Based on images in history books, European slaveholders wore polished black leather boots as a sign of class and nobility. Slaves were barefoot.

I have used the method of image interpretation based on Cynthia Hartzler-Miller's (2001) theory to aid in understanding the slave community. Image interpretation is a historical inquiry approach to assess one's ability to interpret historical evidence and to reconstruct events from the past. Capturing the true essence of my ancestors in bare feet only strengthens my appreciation of their sacrifices.

6
Cornrows

In this chapter we explore Black hair and cornrows as an African cultural custom.

Learning objectives

- To understand the connection between Black hair and Black consciousness.
- To broaden awareness of the cultural roots of Black hair in African and African American tradition.
- To learn about Black hair care as an African tradition.
- To learn about cornrows and hair braiding as a cultural custom in the author's family.

When I looked in the mirror, I saw an African queen, a descendent of slaves, a ruler of my village. As early as at 12 years old, I developed the Black consciousness that my braided hair was a gift from my African ancestors. I came to this realization when the ancestral look of braids and cornrows was likened to that of Cleopatra, Queen of the Ptolemaic Kingdom of Egypt. In the seventh grade in parochial school, I was cast as Cleopatra in a school pageant. For most of my childhood, I wore my hair in braids and cornrows, with beads dangling from my shoulders. While attending this school from the first through eighth grades, I was one of only two Black girls in my class. This exposed me to the prevailing pressures of the Eurocentric views of the world on a daily basis. My little white girlfriends used to tell me that "God was white" and that there were no Black priests in the Catholic church. When I got the part of Cleopatra, I was told that she was white, too. Luckily, owing to the influence of my educated parents and strong Baptist religious background, I did not believe that any of this was true.

Throughout history, Cleopatra has been connected to a variety of identities: Egyptian, Macedonian, African, and Greek. The classic legacy of Cleopatra as an Egyptian is often obscured or omitted from present-day discussions. Most recently, however, the film industry has revived the portrayal of Cleopatra through the lens of the African diaspora. Unfortunately, this has spurred a robust challenge to the idea that Cleopatra is of non-European descent.

My mother and I had to design my costume for the show. All students were required to create their own wardrobe for their characters. To learn more about Cleopatra and her dress designs, my mother and I searched through the encyclopedia. In the mid-1970s, the World Wide Web had not yet been developed; the internet did not exist. In those days, we used the encyclopedia for school projects or to find information on a given topic. We searched for Cleopatra and found several images of her in the book. She was depicted as a white woman wearing a braided wig with diamonds and gold beads. My parents taught me that Egypt was an African country. Therefore, I believed that these Eurocentric images were inaccurate depictions of the queen. My mother was a second-grade school teacher and my father taught high school English literature. What my peers had told me in school contradicted many of my parents' lessons. One of the lessons was to do your own research!

To offer a fun fact: The idea that Egypt was an African country has been challenged throughout our history. Chika Anta Diop, the great scholar and researcher, took on this debate and, through his research studies, determined that Egypt **is** an African country. He drew from anthropology, physics, chemistry, sociology, and linguistics to understand and explain the history of Africa to liberate his people. He used Egyptology to reconnect Egyptian civilization with Africa to demonstrate that Egypt is an African country (Ntongela, 2009). African historiography helped to liberate African culture from dominant colonial historical interpretations (Ntongela, 2009). Through his studies, Diop concluded that Egypt is an African nation. This research has enhanced my appreciation of my cultural connection to the Motherland. Who would have thought that I had my first encounter with an African instrument (the hula hoop) in Brookneal, Virginia, as a little girl!

My mother worked on my hair for hours, trying to duplicate Cleopatra's braiding style shown in the images. However, braiding was not one of her strong skills. Owing to my natural 4C hair type, at times my hair was difficult to manage. My mother sometimes took hours to style my hair. In some African cultures, family members were mostly entrusted with caring for the hair, as this was considered an essential task (White and White, 1995b). My African ancestry is Ghanaian, Masana, and Cameroonian. Byrd and Tharps (2014), in their book *Hair Story: Untangling the Roots of Black Hair in America,* highlighted the intricacies of managing the Black hair of the Cameroon people.

> The complicated and time-consuming task of their hair grooming included washing, combing, oiling, braiding, twisting, and or decorating the hair with any number of adornments including cloth, beads and shells.
>
> (p. 5)

Black hair is my cultural connection to Africa. African women wear coils, cornrows, and knots with braids, which define their role in the African society.

At the parochial school, the white girls used to admire my cornrows. Cornrows were worn by the enslaved in various braided patterns to communicate secret coded messages for those escaping to freedom (Brooks and McNair, 2015). Byrd and Tharps (2014) described the meaning of hair in West African societies:

> In the early 15th century hair acted as a carrier of messages in most West African societies. The citizens of these societies—including the World of Mende, Mandingo, and Yoruba—were the people who filled the slave ships that sailed to the New World.
>
> (p. 2)

Quite frequently, my cousin Jackie came to our house to cornrow my hair. On one occasion, I had gone swimming in the creek the day before. When I woke up that morning, my hair was matted, tangled, and full of tight curls. I could barely comb through it. I washed my hair with detangling shampoo and conditioner. As I scrubbed it, the curls loosened. I brushed it into four sections, so as not to put too much tension on it. Then I let it air dry.

Summers in the South can be very hot. On that day, it was scorching hot outside, muggy, and it rained. In these conditions, my hair style without braids would never last. I selected the hair beads for cousin Jackie to put in my hair. I used to love the clear and white beads, as they looked like the diamonds that Cleopatra wore in the images that I had seen in the encyclopedia.

Cousin Jackie cornrowed my hair in the kitchen. The kitchen is a makeshift hair salon for many Black families. I believe that it became the Black family hub for hairdressing owing to the location of the stove, which was needed for the hot comb or "straightening comb." My mother and grandmother would place the hot comb over the fire and, when it was piping hot, comb through the hair.

Cornrowing hair can be a long, arduous process. When cousin Jackie cornrowed my hair, I had to put a pillow on the chair so that my bum, or "hind pots," as my grandmother used to call it, did not hurt while getting my hair done. The cornrowing process could take up to three or four hours, depending on the style. Sitting still for that period of time can be a painful experience, especially for a young child.

When cousin Jackie removed the four-part sections that I had prepared, I already knew which cornrow design I wanted her to do. She used to part my hair down the middle and crisscross her fingers, creating a flat zig zag braid row by row all over my head. Cousin Jackie braided my hair in different designs. I loved the "updo" or bun style; that was my favorite. When she added beads to my braids, I knew that I was an African queen.

> These laborious hair care rituals were not only essential to a sense of well-being among little Black girls, they were also a part of the many complex survival strategies that African Americans had developed since slavery.
>
> (Rodriguez, 2003, p. 64)

All of my female cousins wore cornrows. The style would stay set for weeks before appearing frizzy or "ratty" from sweating after active play. Although painful at times, the highlight of my summers was spending time with cousin Jackie getting my hair braided. Luckily, cousin Jackie was an expert at cornrowing. At least, she seemed like an expert to me. She was self-taught, with no formal training. Most of us learned how to cornrow by doing each other's hair. This is another common trait for the Black family. To girls, cornrows meant simply a cute hairstyle that kept our hair managed to perfection. Cornrows meant that, for weeks at a time, we did not have to wake up in the morning and do our hair. Cornrows meant that the heat and humidity did not drop the curls. Cornrows meant freedom from heavy hair maintenance for an extended period of time—freedom to swim, freedom to play without worry about messing up your hairstyle, freedom to run outside in the rain and not have to worry about the rain ruining your hairstyle, freedom to get your hair wet in the shower, and freedom to sport your African look for your peers and classmates. For the enslaved, cornrows meant survival, protest, and resistance. Cornrows meant intelligence and skill. Cornrows meant creativeness.

Doing cornrows was a time for bonding. When cousin Jackie cornrowed my hair, we laughed and shared stories about family and life. She was like a big sister to me. Mirroring the images of my enslaved ancestors, my hairstyle is a social ritual. A little Black girl's hair is her glory. You can tell so much about a Black woman just by how she wears her hair: head coverings, cornrows, afros, or shaved heads all have meaning. Hair culture in my family has been modeled after African women's hairstyles. White and White (1995b) argued that,

> In African cultures, the grooming and styling of hair have long been important social rituals. Elaborate hair designs, reflecting tribal affiliation, status, sex, age, occupation, and the like, were common, and the cutting, shaving, wrapping, and braiding of hair were centuries-old arts.

(White and White, 1995b, pp. 49–50)

Black women have an aversion to water touching their hair. In the South, perspiration is a Black girl's enemy. When enslaved women worked the fields, the perspiration dripping from their brows changed the texture of their hair, making it difficult to manage (Brooks and McNair, 2015; Byrd and Tharps, 2014).

When I was growing up, my family did not talk about hair culture as a slave culture. The women in my family had a variety of hair textures, such as 3C, 4A, 4B, and 4C. Before my mother would wash and condition my 4C hair, she would scratch the dandruff from my scalp. Then she would massage a mixture of mayonnaise and eggs into my scalp. It was thick and pasty and had a funny smell. I remember those episodes as if they were yesterday. A comment on fashion and beauty by Ekpenyonganwan (2020), appeared in "The History of the Natural Hair of the African Community," published in Opera News, discusses how Africans used natural hair care products made from environmental herbs.

African women shaved their heads as they mourned the loss of a loved one. African kings had fancy hairstyles, and warriors often braided their hair as they went to war. Life was good and Africans were able to manage and maintain their hair using natural hair products made from herbs found in their environment.

(para. 4)

Until I got my first permanent, my mother struggled to do my hair. I know that many little Black girls can relate to this story. Without a straightening comb or a hair relaxer or chemical straightener, Black hair can be difficult to manage. Generally, mothers choose to perm their little girls' hair after age 12. It was not until I became an adult that I chose to return to my natural hair texture: no perm, no straightening comb, and no hair texturizer. In retrospect, my natural hair and cornrows in my childhood were a bridge to my spiritual connection with my African ancestors.

7
Linguistic Africanisms

In this chapter we explore the history of African American English and the Southern drawl.

Learning objectives

- To broaden awareness of the influence of the African language on the development of African American English and the Southern accent in the South.
- To expand knowledge of common words and phrases that enslaved Africans spoke during the colonial period.
- To facilitate critical thinking about the negative social perceptions of African American English and the southern drawl in the United States.
- To learn how language patterns of the South became a part of American culture.
- To learn about African American English and the Southern drawl as cultural customs in the author's family heritage.

The African American English that the antebellum enslaved African spoke in the South shares common phonological and syntactical features with the English language that my family has spoken for generations. While examining the unpublished manuscript, "Slave Narratives: A Folk History of Slavery in the United States From Interviews With Former Slaves," prepared by The Federal Writers' Project 1936–1938 and assembled by the Library of Congress Project, I discovered idioms and phrases of the formerly enslaved who were interviewed for the project that are reminiscent of the expressions that my grandmother used throughout my life. These records are a collection of two thousand personal historical testimonies obtained through recorded interviews with "ex-slaves" from 17 Southern states.

In these interviews, the formerly enslaved were asked to provide personal testimony about "their attitudes toward one another, toward their masters, mistresses, and overseers, toward poor whites, North and South, the Civil War, Emancipation, Reconstruction, religion, education and virtually every phase of Negro life in the South" (Federal Writers' Project, 1936, p. ix). The documents were eloquently described as an "invaluable body of unconscious evidence or indirect source material, which scholars and writers dealing with the South, especially social psychologists and cultural anthropologists, cannot afford to reckon without" (p. viii). They are not only a compilation of historical testimonial but an original depiction of slave culture in the American South.

Although some scholars have debated the authenticity of such records as not being fully representative of the language spoken by the enslaved African, the archives have provided a basic context for understanding the time and place of African linguistic evolution and development. Mufwene (2015), who categorized slave narratives as "postcolonial documentation," explained the dilemma in accepting narratives as evidence of the actual enslaved African dialect. In his article entitled "The Emergence of African American English," he wrote,

> The other kind of diachronic evidence often adduced to bear on this debate is from the "Ex-Slave Narratives," though they should not be interpreted to reflect faithfully how the former slaves or their descendants actually spoke, as the transcripts were usually edited (Dillard 1973). The basic assumption in the use of these narratives is that which is associated with apparent-time data in discussions of language change (see Labov 1994; Bailey 2002), viz.... . The significance of these texts lies especially in revealing what particular features were then associated with AAE [African American English] at the time the stories were transcribed.
>
> (Mufwene, 2015, p. 67)

The transcripts of the "Slave Narratives" by the Federal Writers' Project indicate that the compilers requested that "authentic dialect" be preserved in their interviews. However, they instructed the interviewers not to "use dialectic spelling 'so complicated' that it may confuse the reader." It also stated that the interviewer should not, "censor any material collected, regardless of its nature" (Federal Writers' Project, 1936, p. xx). Mr. John A. Lomax, the National Advisor on Folklore and Folkways for the Federal Writers' Project at the time, wrote to Mr. George Cronyn, the Associate Director, Federal Writer's Project, "I much prefer to read unedited (but typed) "interviews" (Federal Writers' Project, 1936, p. xv). Furthermore, the transcript indicates that the following instructions were noted: "The details of the interview should be reported as accurately as possible in the language of the original statement" (Federal Writers' Project, 1936, p. xxii) and Mr. Lomax described in his letter to Mr. Cronyn, "All the interviews should copy the 'Negro expressions'" (p. xv). Thus, it is evident that these Slave Narratives depict in some manner the "original" language of the formerly enslaved in their own words.

Scholars have also questioned whether linguistic Africanisms survived over time in North America. Holloway (2005) defined Africanisms as "elements of culture in the New World which can be traced to an African origin" (p. 2). Scholars have determined that "African cultural influences" continued to persist in the American colonies and were preserved by the enslaved African communities through inheritance and tradition (Baugh, 1999; Brown and de Casanova, 2014; Herskovits, 1938; Holloway and Vass, 1997). The African American language has endured and established a permanency in American culture (Baugh, 1999; Holloway and Vass, 1997, p. xv).

The Virginia colonies, the place of the inception of my Southern ancestral roots, are central to understanding the emergence of African American Vernacular English (AAVE). According to Rawley (1991, as cited in Mufwene, 2015, p. 60), Virginia is key to unearthing the roots of the English language in America.

> Virginia is critical to understanding the evolution of English in the United States because it provided the founder slave population for second-generation colonies such as North Carolina, which would develop on its model rather than on that of South Carolina.

In my investigation into colonial slave dialectic, it became apparent that my ancestral connection to this linguistic African culture was no longer uncertain. These revelations are eye opening and have heightened my intellectual curiosity to explore further my family's use of African American English.

An example of the African cultural linguistic derivative that my family inherited is the Southern accent. My grandmother and other family members who live in the South and even those who migrated to the North speak with a Southern accent. The Southern accent has persisted throughout African American and American culture for generations, despite changes in the environment and demography (Amira et al., 2018; Brown and de Casanova, 2014; Cade, 1935; Gehrmann, 2007). Schaffer (2005) suggested that the Southern accent is a combination of African dialects that has sustained its power over American culture for generations. In his book *Bound to Africa: The Mandinka Legacy in the New World,* he wrote,

> I propose that the Southern accent, despite all its varieties, is essentially an African-American slave accent, and possibly a Mandinka accent, with other African accents, along with the colonial British accent layered in.

(p. 322)

Despite its historical significance, the Southern accent in America has been associated with "negative stereotypes" (Amira et al., 2018; Cumming, 1959; Dillard, 1973; Gehrmann, 2007; Lanehart, 2001). Holloway (2005) spoke of how "the languages of the African people were denigrated and characterized as mumbo jumbo" (p. 398). I was naive to think that my grandmother's African American English and Southern accent were manifestations of her limited education, poor socioeconomic background, and farm life. However, I have unearthed the significance of linguistic Africanisms on the acculturation of my family.

Childhood memory

I was an inquisitive child. My curiosity about Grandmother Cathy's life experiences began at a very early age. Frequently, I questioned her about being raised on a farm in Virginia and how this experience had contributed to the woman whom she had become. I would argue that her lived experience influenced tremendously who I am as an African American woman of Southern roots, as I inherited her family traditions.

Her mother, my great-grandmother, passed away when Cathy was a little girl. Cathy could not seem to recall her age when great-grandma died. She did indicate that it was well before her teenage years, sometime after her youngest sister was born. Cathy's father, my great-grandfather, raised her and her eight siblings on the farm. He took on the roles and responsibilities of mother and father owing to the death of his wife so early on. Despite the difficult times that they had, like many Black families during this time, my great-grandfather made sure that his children were secure and loved.

I recall the personal accounts that my grandmother, born in 1921, shared about her educational experiences in the early twentieth century. She attended school only to the fourth or fifth grade. Back then, it was commonplace for Black children in the South to complete only an elementary education. Owing to institutional discrimination, schooling, especially in the deep rural areas of the South, was almost nonexistent for African American children. My family did not escape this circumstance. I later realized that it was erroneous on my part to believe that my grandmother's

African American English was solely the product of a lack of education; instead, it stemmed from African linguistic tradition of my enslaved ancestors. Slaveholders mocked the linguistic capabilities of Africans and questioned their intelligence (Farrison, 1977; Gehrmann, 2007; Holloway and Vass, 1997; Johnson, 2000; Kohn, 2005).

Grandma Cathy and her eight siblings attended school in a little gray schoolhouse built from wooden scraps and splintered gray shingles. The structure remains today. Like most schools in the South during that time, the system for African American children was severely underfunded. There was a shortage of books, blackboards, and desks. The classroom was one small room. The teacher was a woman from the local African American church. There was no public transportation. Children of mixed ages were taught in one "classroom."

Years later, my great-uncle (my grandmother's older brother) purchased the schoolhouse to use as a primary residence. This little gray schoolhouse is a legacy in my family. He and his wife raised their two children, my cousins, in this house for all of their lives. I used to visit them there every summer from childhood through adulthood until my uncle and aunt passed away. My cousins still own the property. There was an outhouse in the back yard. It fascinated me, but I became accustomed to it and used it for most of my childhood. My great aunt and great-uncle could not afford to install indoor plumbing. After my uncle died, when I was about 11 or 12 years old, my aunt installed a bathroom near the kitchen on the first floor of the house. The property is historical, as it represents the time and place of the acculturation of my grandmother and her siblings during their formative years.

My grandmother lived in a brick house about a mile down the road from the schoolhouse. Following her death, my mother and I cleaned out her residence. In the process of clearing cabinets and drawers, I came across her Bibles with handwritten notes, stored in cabinets and dressers throughout the house—in the kitchen, bathroom, and bedrooms. Cathy was a religious and spiritual woman. When I read her little notes, I noticed that they were prayers that she had written. These notes were evidence of her African linguistic tradition. Some phrases were, "I pray to Lawd" (I prayed to the Lord), "I readin' a book 'bout deLawd" (I am reading a book about the Lord), and "I know'd dis befo" (I knew this before). She used "dis" (this) and "dat" (that), and "wit" (with). According to Holloway (2005), these are examples of grammatical patterns similar to those of Niger-Congo languages and are evidence that support the idea that African American English has "preserved its African linguistic character" (p. 418).

Another example from The Federal Writers' Project (1936) was a transcript of an interview with Ms. Lula Flannigan, a formerly enslaved woman who was 78 years old at the time: "All de white folks love ter see plenty er healthy, strong black chillum comin' long, en dey wuz watchful ter see dat 'omans had good keer when dey chilluns wuz bawned" (p. xxiv). Ms. Flannigan's testimony brought tears to my eyes. This connection is so powerful, as Cathy used those same words: "de" (they), "ter" (to), "chillum" and "chilluns" (children), "comin'" (coming), "wuz" (was), and "bawned" (born).

Many days, my grandmother and her five sisters would sit around the dining room table, laughing and talking, using these very same words and phrases, in their Southern way. These documents are a trail of clues to my grandmother's use of African American English.

One afternoon, my great-uncle pulled up in my grandmother's driveway in his pick-up truck. When I looked out of the window, I saw him wearing his overalls and work boots, walking up to the side door. I suspected that he had just finished working in the tobacco field. He worked on our family farm six days a week, with the exception of Sundays, which was a day for church and rest. He is one of Grandma Lene's (the owner of the "Big House") twin sons. He was born and raised on our tobacco plantation on the "Big House" property.

In the South (or "country," as we would call it), when guests came over, it was like Christmas day because the pace is normally slow. A visitor was a major event! I answered the door. He was chewing tobacco, dripping from the side of his mouth. He greeted my grandmother, in his Southern way, with a smile. He embraced us with a warm hug. He explained where he had been that day: "Yeah, great day! I's rollin' Roberts way fo' to catch me so' fish."

This was music to my ears. Fascinating! When my great-uncle and grandmother spoke, it sounded like they were singing. It is difficult to describe. It was as if they were speaking another language.

My mother, born and raised in the South, communicates with him in that way, too. His deep Southern accent made it difficult for me to understand exactly what he was saying. However, my mother, who is arguably a true "Southern belle," was able to understand perfectly. Having been born and raised on the farm, she discerned the strong Southern accent. Exactly how that influenced me is another story.

My family members who remained in the South have a strong Southern drawl. My mother migrated to the North soon after graduating from college at the age of 23. She retained many Southern traditions, including the Southern accent. Her Southern roots definitely had an influence on me. Throughout my life, I was told that I pronounce certain words with that Southern "twang." However, I never truly explored the tenacity of my Southern ways; I only listened to what others had to say. Friends and strangers alike would say, "You speak with a Southern accent" and "you act like a Southern girl." Growing up, it was a natural phenomenon.

The Southern accent is one of the most identifiable accents in the country (Amira et al., 2018). The Southern drawl has evolved in various ways, depending on the part of the country in which one resides. The varieties can be traced back to the establishment of the British colonies (Amira et al., 2018; Cumming, 1959). The differences between the accents of the northern and southern regions of the country became more apparent after the Civil War (Amira et al., 2018, Cumming, 1959; Dillard, 1973; Gehrmann, 2007). The migration of Blacks to the North resulted in racist and discriminatory policies, and social unrest became more prevalent.

The breakdown of the slave system and the perceived economic, political, and religious freedom in the North served as factors for the African American migration to northern cities, beginning in the late 1860s. Some of my own family members migrated to the North during the early 1900s, chiefly to Monmouth County, New Jersey. They took with them Southern cultural practices that they had learned on the Virginia farms.

In *Dark Ghetto,* Kenneth Clark makes an interesting observation as he argues that forces such as economic, political, and religious freedoms were "essentially [those] of a colony" (as cited in Blauner, 1969, p. 394). Northern manufacturing, challenged by a lack of European immigrant laborers owing to the First World War and ensuing restrictive immigration laws, lured Blacks from the Southern plantation by offering high pay for work in the North. My maternal grandmother Cathy, who was forced to leave the South owing to employment limitations, moved to Monmouth County, New Jersey, and worked in a sewing factory in the hope of a better financial future.

The Jim Crow segregation laws meant diminishing opportunities in agrarian labor in the South for her and for many Black families. This had an impact on the economic conditions of the maternal side of the family. These repressive laws excluded many of my maternal family members, including my grandmother, from the Southern plantation system and forced them to seek industrial opportunities in the North.

In general, most of the African American migration to northern cities began around the 1890s (Foreman, 2017; Osofsky, 1966, p. 19). My maternal grandmother moved to the North in the late 1960s, while my mother was attending college in the South. Her oldest sister and two brothers had already moved to the North. Although a small number of African Americans were already living in northern cities, the majority migrated from the South during this period (Foreman, 2017). This was true for many Black families during this time. The rapid demographic shift continued during and even after the First World War. This migration of Blacks significantly shifted the distribution of the African American population in the United States. Despite this shift, the Southern accent of Blacks and whites remained similar or the same (Amira et al., 2018; Mufwene, 2015; Pollitzer, 1999). This is significant because, although race relations were unsettled in most states, the common cultural bond of language existed in the northern and southern regions of the United States.

Cathy, my maternal grandmother, who lived in the South for most of her life, could never properly pronounce my first name, Deirdre (pronounced phonetically as Dee-i-dra). I was affectionately known to her as "Deatrice" (pronounced dee-a-triss). My uncle, who never left the South, also mispronounced my name; he, like my grandma Lene, called me "De-at-ra." Most of my family members in the South and those who migrated to the North call me "De-at-ra" with a Southern drawl. Knowing that my family's English language patterns are similar or in some cases the same as those of enslaved Africans is a blessing to cherish for a lifetime.

Mufwene (2015) endorsed the notion that the English dialect evolved out of slave culture.

> I submit that the Africans definitely shaped the varieties now associated with their descendants in the New World by selecting from within English those features that were congruent with those of some of the languages they had spoken in Africa (Corne 1999), by modifying the characteristics of some of the English options they selected, or by introducing new features (identified as "apports" by Allsopp 1977; see also Mufwene 2001a, b).
>
> (Mufwene, 2015, p. 57)

Every year, when I would visit down South, I had to become acclimated to the sounds and rhythms of the Southern African American English. My grandmother, uncles, and cousins, all born, bred, and raised on the tobacco farm, seemed to speak a different language altogether. When I was very young, I would sit and watch their mouths move and try to make out what they were saying; I soon grew accustomed to it. It was much stronger than my mother's accent, so I had to adjust. I was eventually able to understand their style of communication.

Cumming (1959) discussed the speech of Southerners in his article, "Eatonton's Southern Accent":

> There are remnants of the vigorous speech of the frontiersmen, the vernacular of the slaves rich with overtones from their spirituals and folk-songs, the deep and angry murmur of outraged patriots, the flute-like conversation of elegant ladies, the cotton buyer's jargon, the evangelist's exhortations, the dialect of the critters flowing and slurring artlessly together.
>
> (p. 207)

Slave dialect is not a remnant of the past but a staple of the present and reinvention for the future (Baugh, 1999; Brown and de Casanova, 2014; Cade, 1935; Cumming, 1959; Dillard, 1973). The Southern drawl is historically rooted in slave culture. My grandmother's accent was distinct in nature, with her merging words. Every word spilled into the next, like the sound of a hummingbird. I could snap my fingers to the beat of her sound! It is intriguing to think that the slave dialect remains in families for generations.

An example of this is what I encountered one day at the corner store. I awoke early one Saturday morning and decided to go shopping at the country store down the road from my grandmother's house. Not caring much about my appearance, I wore my pink cotton pajama pants, white T-shirt, flip flops, and a head scarf. The Southern culture encourages a relaxed atmosphere. Down South, there is a tendency not to care about how one is dressed or about the condition of one's hair styles in certain settings.

I grabbed my grandmother's car keys and off I went to the Red House Market. I entered the store and the attendant greeted me with the Southern drawl. He was of Asian descent. But this should not be surprising if he was raised in the South. The other customers who entered the store were white and greeted me with a Southern accent as well. The language patterns of the South were adopted by all races. The Southern accent had become a part of American culture.

Enslaved people contributed to the creation of a language legacy, a language culture that reached all who occupied the South. I would argue that the generational sustainment of African languages developed a strong common bond among Southerners. On the plantation, the enslaved communicated with each other with affection and familiarity.

I end with a poem that I wrote when I began this chapter:

> African dialect and European British tones
> A mix of languages is the root of my favor
> Lucky to be a southern girl
> A culture that can't be denied

So evident so clear so crystal in my mind
Yet soulful and diverse
Can it be that it's not a curse
Embrace it softly recognize its truth
For sake of commonality we are all connected

Conclusion

My travels to Ghana destroyed any prior romanticization of the gruesome realities of the transatlantic slave trade and slavery that might have formed in my mind since childhood. Visiting the slave dungeons, standing in the physical space, provided a visual and spiritual revelation that was something that I could see, touch, and feel as I tried to grasp the realities of the horrific encounters of this era. Like many others, the first time that I had ever seen a depiction of slavery was when I was about 10 years old, watching the made-for-television movie *Roots*. From that point on, I became socially conscious and aware of my African ancestry and the institution of slavery on the Southern plantation in the United States. With my family "roots" in the South, I connected my ancestry to the enslaved with mild uncertainty but without doubt. These images left a lasting impression, culminating in a burning desire to learn about Africa and my connection to my African ancestors in the Americas and throughout the African diaspora.

White resistance to African customs and traditions enabled my ancestors to create their own cultural dynasty on the Southern plantation. On a daily basis, my enslaved ancestors lived in fear for their lives, health, safety, and well-being. Despite these obstacles, some figuratively constructed a wall of protection to maintain their self-awareness and self-identity of their native homeland. While some found it more beneficial to assimilate into the culture of their enslavers, some strove to retain their African cultural difference for the independence and freedom of their human souls. Others established practices for survival. The Southern plantation was essentially a space to build cultural capital in the enslaved community. This cultural capital is my family's legacy.

My mind is overflowing with profound memories and recollections that have inspired this journey of self-awareness. When I was a young child, the only images of enslaved people that I witnessed were in children's books, which depicted them as "happy-go-lucky" servants. My mother read books to me about Black history. A second-grade school teacher, she made books a staple in our household. I recall seeing an enslaved woman dressed in a full-length blue floral skirt with a long white apron, black boots, and a white cloth wrapped around her head. She was smiling as she carried a pail of water from a well. Yes! In the image, she was SMILING! I rarely saw images of enslaved women with their hair exposed to public view. It seemed that Black hair was consistently hidden under scarfs or wraps. This explains in part my motivation to include a chapter on Black hair in this study, to highlight the beauty of our Black physical traits that have historically been assigned a cruel interpretation. When my son was in elementary school in the mid-2000s, his history book depicted enslaved people in a similar manner. Time has not changed these misrepresentations and denials of African heritage and Black culture.

I looked out from the porch of the "Big House" onto the 500 acres that my great-grandfather had inherited and owned and operated, wondering what the field was trying to tell me. One can only imagine the history of my ancestors' Southern lives on these fields.

The job of the enslaver was to inflict the enslaved with psychological and physical abuse in order to control their minds. The aim was to dismantle any thought of individuality, ancestral practices, and self-identity in order to control their "property" completely. But, when standing in the field, looking out to the endless rows of nature, I could feel the spirit of my African ancestors celebrating their sense of freedom—freedom to stay connected to their homeland through cultural practices and tradition. Even under the harshest circumstances, their human spirit could not be broken. This has generationally only strengthened the Black family. Despite the dehumanization imposed on my enslaved ancestors by their enslavers, the ancestral spirit conveys to me that they did not ever lose their consciousness of being human— human, with a mind, feelings, ideas, and the legacy of culture. The transportation of the customs and traditions from their native land gave them the silent power of strength, endurance, and survival. How might such a legacy remain? I wrote this poem to express my feelings on sustaining my heritage:

> The human spirit. The human soul.
> So powerful on earth. So powerful to know.
> Holding on to nature's grip. A strong will and mind
>   won't slip.
> I sit and wonder for minutes at a time.
> Thoughts of my enslaved ancestors choke me with
>   emotion.
> I ask myself, "What does it mean to be enslaved?"
> The operative word: enslaved.
> Does it mean to erase all memory of your
>   former self,

culture, customs and traditions from your
    homeland?
Does it mean to submit to forced
    acculturation and
assimilation in a strange land?
Does it mean to forget that you ever existed in
    another time or place?
I sometimes wonder: If it weren't for their power
    of brilliance and wisdom, would the enslaved
    African have been able to sustain
the African traditions, the legacy that it has
    maintained?

Ever since I was a little girl, I questioned my cultural heritage and the connections to the enslaved African. Where did it come from? My maternal grandmother Cathy shared many stories about our family traditions. I knew that, as an African American, I had a culture. But was it African or was it American? Unfortunately, too many of us are unaware of the cultural Africanisms in our families that are our legacy. We **are** legacy! Something invaluable and precious to behold. African culture was incorporated into European culture to create an "American culture." Whites in the South embraced and practiced African customs, but without offering acknowledgment or giving credit where credit was due.

I helped my grandmother Cathy to write a speech for her to read at one of our family reunions. In my opinion, this is an expression of her dignity and pride in our family heritage.

I like to make an input about my mom and dad being a Black American. Marcelius and Elizabeth were my dad and mom. There were 10 children in our family. And they raised a foster child. My mother died at an early age. My father was an industrial and businessman. He was a farmer. He owned his own farm. He owned his business: a sawmill—the only Black man owning a business in Charlotte County and surrounding counties. He hired many men to work for him. He helped our race, putting food on many people's tables. In the later years, when he gave up saw milling, he owned a community store, where people came and enjoyed themselves, keeping up with the community news. I helped my father, took care of his business. Dad said, "If your business don't bother you, keep on sleeping." My dad was a Christian man and a member of White Oak Grove Church. These are words of wisdom! You can quickly lose interest in "war-ship" if you have nothing invested. This is what has made me the person that I am today, because of my dad! *Thank you, Lord. Thank you!*

When I read this speech, I feel her heartfelt pride. I cherish this letter because, as depicted in the film *Summer Bee,* there is much history in the South. However, at Charlotte Courthouse, most of the legal documents have been lost or not preserved owing to the racist history of slavery and Jim Crow in the South. The birth certificates and other precious documents were never created or archived. Therefore, this letter presents to me a significant historical artifact of my family story.

Tracing my family's cultural roots was difficult. When one is raised in one's culture, one does not consider the value of those experiences in the time that they happen. While I am living in my culture, I am not conscious of it. I teach my son the memories of our family legacy because a sense of our family history and our ancestral roots is critical to his identity. It is the true essence of life.

Let us remember the gospel song, "mine eyes have seen the glory of the coming of the lord," also known as the "Battle Hymn of the Republic," written by abolitionist Julia Ward Howe in 1861. The song provides me with hope that, one day, our nation will join together to seek a broader and fuller understanding of the truth behind American cultural history, cultural roots, and cultural heritage.

Recommended discussion topics

1. In what ways does the concept "slave culture" apply to American culture?

2. How can you apply the author's multidimensional explanatory model to your own cultural background and experiences? Please give specific examples.

3. How did slavery impact the cultural practices of enslaved Africans on the Southern plantation?

4. Name at least five cultural traditions that your family practices that are common to African traditions and/or to those of enslaved Africans in America. How have these cultural customs created a system of support and cooperation in your family and in the community? How can these customs be maintained in your family?

5. What is the significance of the Southern plantation in the American South? How did plantation life contribute to the creation of American culture? How did the plantation contribute to racial casting in the enslaved community?

6. What actions can we Americans take to challenge and end cultural racism?

7. What does the term "cultural assimilation" mean?

8. What does the term "minority group" mean? Give an example of a minority group in American society (e.g., Latino/a, female identified). How can you identify with the characterization: "minority group."

9. Why are African traditions so common to American culture but not often discussed or taught in schools?

10. Explain the concept of the word "race." Is "race" real or a socially constructed concept? What is the historical significance of the word? How has society placed value on the social concept of "race"?

11. What is the historical significance of African American English and the Southern accent, as they relate to American culture?

Appendix: A multidimensional theoretical model

In this section, I present a multidimensional explanatory model of African American cultural identity from slavery to modern-day oppression through a discussion of slavery, internal colonization, colonialism, Noel (1968) and Blauner's hypothesis, minority group status, paternalism, opposition collective identity, W. E. B. Du Bois's theory of double consciousness, the theory of racism proposed by Brondolo et al. (2012) and Jones (1997), and Pierre Bourdieu's theory of social reproduction.

Learning objectives

- To learn various theoretical concepts that can be applied to understanding African American cultural identity.
- To raise awareness of the African American status as a minority in the United States through centuries of oppression and marginalization.
- To broaden knowledge of slavery in the North Americas.

Slavery

I begin this discussion with a brief analysis of American slavery. Slavery was one of the most profitable institutions in United

States history, yet it is overlooked and insufficiently examined. As a descendant of enslaved Africans, my cultural identity has been shaped by the forced migration of my African ancestors to the plantations of Virginia. Slavery, one of history's most cruel and destructive institutions, can be traced back to early civilization, prior to the establishment of the American colonies. It has been practiced in all parts of the world.

The first 20 Africans arrived in the British colonies at Jamestown, Virginia, in 1619. The initial labor system of the English "New World" was an indentured servitude system, which allowed the person who paid for the cost of another's passage/travel from England to the colonies to enjoy the fruits of that person's labor for five to seven years to pay off the debt.

In the next few decades in the British colonies, slavery became an institutionalized form of bondage by which a person was considered someone's property for life. The plantation system expanded as white indentured servitude decreased owing to indentured laborers' abandonment of their creditors' properties and the general return migration of Europeans to their homelands. As a result, the enslaved African became the main source of labor. The Europeans attempted to enslave American Indians, who inhabited the Americas when they arrived. However, the natives' knowledge of the terrain and the severe decrease in their population owing to warfare, death, and disease made their enslavement impractical.

In the slave systems established by the English, Spanish, Dutch, and Portuguese to build the economic infrastructure for their colonies, the enslaved were unpaid and exploited. From 1619 to 1807, more than 500,000 slaves were transported by force through the transatlantic slave trade to the British colonies (the United States of America, following the Revolutionary War of 1776; Baker, 1998.) Most of the enslaved came from West-Central Africa. Slaves came to colonial Virginia by more than one route, which enabled the colony to secure its captives for the cultivation of crops and other agricultural needs. Slaves were imported from the African continent, from the West Indies by way of Africa, and from other British mainland colonies (Kulikoff, 2012). Research indicates that the number of slaves imported into Virginia from 1699 to April 1727 was 22,897 (Kulikoff, 2012). This time period is important to me because, through my research, I found that many of my ancestors lived in Virginia during that time.

Although slavery had long existed in certain parts of Africa, that system was different from the system in the United States. In Africa, a person would become enslaved owing to a loss during warfare among African villages. The village that lost the war had to pay a debt to their conquerors. The debt was paid through the enslavement of the conquered. In many cases, once the enslaved person's debt was paid, they were set free or became part of the family of their former enslaver (Du Bois, 1903; Herbert, 1970). In the United States, however, the enslaved had no rights; they were considered as chattel or personal property of the slaveholder, which meant that they could be owned for life. They were viewed by the Europeans as "savages"; not considered to be human. Their cultural, physical, and racial differences from the English people made them a peculiar curiosity in the English mind. As Winthrop Jordan (1974) put it, "Negroes looked different to Englishmen, their religion was un-Christian; their manner of living was anything but English; they seemed to be a particularly libidinous sort of people" (p. 4; see also Foreman, 2017). Africans were distinct in skin complexion, hair type, religious practices, value systems and morals, language patterns, government, culture, and customs, which elicited feelings of contempt from the slaveholders. In America, the initial contact between English settlers (colonizer) and Africans (colonized group) transpired through labor and servitude.

During the early seventeenth century, the contact between European colonists and Africans contributed to a racialized social system that benefited British colonists and served to the detriment of Africans and American Indians. Arnold Sio argued that there was "discrimination against the Negro before the slave status was fully defined and before Negro labor became pivotal to the economic system" (Smedley and Smedley, 2012, p. 98).

Although the transatlantic slave trade and the importation of Africans to the United States legally ended in 1808, enslaved Africans born in the United States were not considered to be US citizens until the ratification of the Fourteenth Amendment in 1868, three years after the signing of the Emancipation Proclamation on January 1, 1863.

Millions of enslaved Africans were brought from Central-West Africa to the New World. By the late 1820s, more than two million Africans were living in bondage in the United States (Campbell, 2007). Slaveholders had complete control over the lives of their "property" and the children born to them.

Northern colonies used the enslaved in all aspects of industry. For example, enslaved Africans were widely used in the textile industry, cotton mills, fishing, coal mines, and railroads, which transformed the northern region into a dominant economic force. In 1740, one-fifth of New York City's population was enslaved (Allison et al., 2021; McManus, 2001b). Following the Revolutionary War, many Northern states quickly passed laws to abolish slavery. Slavery ended in Massachusetts around 1780. New York passed gradual emancipation laws in 1799; by 1840, no slaves were listed in the New York census (Allison et al., 2021; Blatt and Roediger, 2018; McManus, 2001a). New Jersey passed an act to emancipate slave children born after July 4, 1804. However, the state did not outlaw slavery until 1865 (Cooley, 1896).

The Southern states continued to rely on the enslaved to work on the plantations and in all aspects of the Southern economy. Unlike the North, the South fought to keep slavery legal in order to continue to reap economic benefits afforded to the South. The use of unpaid workers with no freedom made the Southern states rich and powerful.

Slavery supported the US economy in significant ways. The invention of the cotton gin in 1793 led to massive increases in cotton production, making slavery indispensable to both the Northern and Southern states. The free manual labor of the enslaved, coupled with a machine that could separate the seeds from the cotton ball and therefore produce cotton at high speed, made slavery critical to the development of North America.

The value of the enslaved was determined by the amount of labor that a slave could generate, minus maintenance costs (the slave's food, clothing, housing) over his or her lifetime. The enslaved were bought and sold at slave auctions. Buyers carefully considered the slave's health, physical condition, age, gender, job skills, and anticipated work output.

Although Abraham Lincoln signed the Emancipation Proclamation in 1863, only 3.1 million of the nation's 4 million enslaved Africans were freed. Slavery did not actually end until December 6, 1865 with the ratification of the Thirteenth Amendment.

Internal colonization and colonialism

This section introduces colonial theories, specifically the theories of internal colonization and colonialism, to understand the racial hierarchy that African Americans had to navigate in the United States. Historically, sociologists, anthropologists, and historians have applied the model of colonization and colonialism to the examination of African Americans throughout the Americas (Foreman, 2017; Hind, 1984; Lee and Cho, 2012). The colonial status of African Americans helps to understand African American cultural identity. Eldridge Cleaver said, "Any analysis which does not acknowledge the colonial status of black people cannot hope to deal with the real problem" (as cited in Hind, 1984, p. 546; see also Foreman, 2017).

In order to understand colonialism, an examination must take place of the condition under which the group comes into contact with the colonizer. Generally, this theory has been applied to the study of racially, politically, economically, and socially disenfranchised groups in the United States (Bogdanowicz et al., 2003; Foreman, 2017). The application of colonial theories to the study of internal racial developments in the United States was popular in the 1960s. According to Reinhard (2001), colonization is a neutral term referring to migration to an established settlement, often an agrarian society. By contrast, modern colonization, or the "colonial complex," is described by Kortright (2003) as having the following components: (a) the colonizing power's distortion or destruction of indigenous cultures, (b) the forced, involuntary power; (c) the governing of the colonized population/s by representatives of the colonizing group, and (d) the buttressing of the dominant-subordinate hierarchy by a racist ideology (Foreman, 2017; Kortright, 2003).

Reinhard (2001) argued that colonialism involves control and exploitation of differences in order to ensure the economic, political, and cultural domination of one group over another. According to Reinhard (2001, p. 2240), there are three types of colonies: "trade and military bases; colonies of settlement; [and] colonies of exploitation." The English introduced slavery into their North American colonies to use them for both settlement and exploitation (Foreman, 2017; Reinhard, 2001).

Omi and Winant (2004) offer a "colonial analysis" of American race relations that explores the idea of white-Black relations in America as essentially those of "colonizer" and "colonized." They juxtapose the African American community in the United States and the continents of Africa and Asia as politically, economically, and militarily subordinate to white America and the continents of Africa and Asia.

However, according to Allen et al. (1998), colonies do not have to exist externally; they can also exist within a given country. Colonization is related to migration and the movement of people from one part of the world to another to establish a settlement (Memmi, 2013).

Blauner (1969) explained the distinction between colonization and colonialism: Colonization, "as a process, is distinguished from colonialism as an economic and political social system in order to isolate the common features in the experience and situation of Afro-Americans and the colonial peoples" (p. 393). This concept can be applied when examining the racial developments that African Americans have had to navigate in the United States.

Pablo Gonzales Casanova is considered the first to have used the term "internal colonialism" in the context of a distinct form of colonization (Hind, 1984). According to Casanova, North American colonization took a form that is distinct from that of other societies. America's is considered to be a form of colonization distinctive from that of the process that takes place in an international capacity (Omi and Winant, 2004). Casanova attempted to integrate the concepts of caste, racism, ethnicity, culture, and economic exploitation into an overall conceptual model (Casanova, 1965).

Similarly, Malcolm X's perception of the white-Black paradigm was that African Americans were a "colonized group" in the United States (Breitman and Morrison, 1966). Allen (2005) traces the historical evolution of this concept of domestic colonialism to colonized group formation in America. Allen (2005) acknowledges W. E. B. Du Bois for his contributions to the theoretical movement of internal colonialism. He highlights that Du Bois spoke of the status of "Negroes" as "nothing more than a colonial status" (p. 2). Harold Cruse (1960), another internal colonialism theorist, wrote in *Revolutionary Nationalism and the Afro-American* that, "from the beginning, the American Negro has existed in the United States as a colonial being" (p. 2). In tracing this concept well into the

1960s (post Du Bois), the examination of the African American in American society remained consistent.

Theories of colonization and colonialism as they related to African American culture have been an integral part of twentieth- and early twenty-first-century political discourse throughout the world.

The contact situation

The condition under which groups make initial contact results in one group assuming a minority status in society and the relationship between the groups can continue in this pattern for generations (Healey and O'Brien, 2014). According to Donald Noel (1968), sociologists developed the theory based on conditions in which the contact situation is characterized by ethnocentrism, competition, and a differential in power that can produce inequality and social stratification. Ethnocentrism is seeing one's own group (the "in" group) as righteous and superior, one's own standards of value as universal, and the standards of other groups as inferior, according to the standard of one's own group (Hammond and Axelrod, 2006, p. 926; Healy and O'Brien, 2014; Hooghe, 2008; Noel, 1968). Competition is the process of trying to overcome or make gains over another group in terms of employment, housing, and educational opportunities (Healey et al., 2018). Differential power is the power that accompanies one group's occupational authority over another group (Barstow, 2008).

Historians, cultural anthropologists, and sociologists have applied all three elements to the study of colonialism and slavery. For example, ethnocentrism played a significant role in the domination of colonial societies by Europeans and their placement of Africans in an inferior status based on their perceived lack of cultural history (Hooghe, 2008). Competition over land and labor existed among English settlers, American Indians, Africans, and white indentured servants. Differential power can be applied to the act of enslavement of Africans.

According to Healey et al. (2018), American Indians militarily outmaneuvered the English colonists over time, which was one of the major reasons they escaped enslavement. As laws became more codified, the distinction between white indentured servants and African indentured servants became evident. Gradually, the laws of white versus African indentured servitude and chattel slavery became more harsh. White indentured servants, who were mostly of Irish descent, were subjected to labor law that was much less harsh than were African servants. The legalization of the enslavement of African captives was an act that legitimatized the power differential between free and unfree people. Based on this system of labor, this population could negotiate their terms of labor and would therefore be assigned less harsh labor under the law (Anderson, 2012). Africans, on the other hand, fit the "Blauner hypothesis" as a forced colonized group with distinct physical and cultural characteristics who could be coerced into enslavement and therefore did not possess the bargaining power to escape this system of oppression (Kendall, 2012). Dominant-minority relations in the United States have engendered this history of oppression.

Dimensions of minority group status

African Americans are a forced colonized group that has been coerced into an involuntary minority group status (Healey and O'Brien, 2014). According to Smith (1991), identity development is a life-long process that is strengthened or weakened by one's majority/minority status. Smith proposed the identity development model to explain why certain groups experience inequality and others experience advantage. The dominant group is defined by numeric representation and/or a position of power in society. On the other hand, to understand the significance of what it means to be a member of a minority group, it must be seen to have distinctive dimension. According to Wagley and Harris (1958), certain characteristics distinguish a minority group from the dominant group in society: (a) experiences with societal disadvantage, inequality, and/or discrimination; (b) common physical features, culture, and language; (c) self-awareness of their status or social identity; (d) involuntary membership in the minority group, with membership assumed at birth; and (e) established social and cultural capital in the group—kinships, friendships, marriages (Healey and O'Brien, 2014; Wagley and Harris, 1958). The minority group status and physical and cultural identities are imposed by the dominant group in society. At times, owing to the negative connotation associated with minority group membership (e.g., slavery, Jim Crow, lower intelligence, laziness), members may denounce their own culture and heritage based on its rejection by the dominant group. This "rejection" may result not only from the dominant group but also from family and friends within their own group (Wagley and Harris, 1958).

Prejudice, racism, and discrimination have contributed to the creation and maintenance of minority group status in the United States and denial of the enslaved African's cultural contributions to American society. Once this concept is created through dominant group bias, partiality, and prejudice, the worldview and shared ideological perspectives of the minority group can be sustained for centuries.

Colonized groups are forced into minority status by the dominant group at the initial "contact situation" between the two groups (Healey et al., 2018). The status problems are the external forces that mark the population because they were enslaved and burdened with a clear distinction of inferiority. In *Still the Big News: Racial Oppression in America,* Bob Blauner (2001) argues that, as a result of terms of their initial contact with Europeans, the status of African Americans has been defined by enslavement and **assaults on their beliefs and culture**. Slaveholders prohibited their slaves from practicing certain Africa customs, such as their native religion, cooking their own foods, or singing and dancing to African songs. Enslaved Africans were considered members of a group, regardless of self-identification (Fordham and Ogbu, 1986).

Similarly, John Ogbu argued that African Americans are considered to be a colonized minority group in America (Gibson and Ogbu, 1991). Robert Blauner (1969) described the distinction between the concepts of colonization as a process and colonialism as a social, economic, and political system to capture the realities of the slave colonies in North America.

Paternalism

Paternalism is relevant to the development of the plantation system, where enslaved Africans lived, worked, and created a "culture of survival." A land- and slave-owning elite in a plantation-based economy that established a type of dominant-minority relationship is often referred to as "paternalism" (McGary, 1998). Healey et al. (2018) explained that the key features of paternalism are "vast power differentials and huge inequalities between dominant and minority groups, elaborate and repressive systems of control over the minority group, caste-like barriers between groups, elaborate and highly stylized codes of behavior and communication between groups, and low rates of overt conflict" (p. 107).

However, a range of scholars disagree with the characterizations of slavery as a paternalistic system. For example, Howard McGary (1998), in *Paternalism and Slavery,* called into question this notion and concluded that slavery was not merely unjust, underserved, and unreasonable (p. 188) but a patently wicked system. Still, upon closer examination, slavery can be viewed as a paternalistic system as it required childlike, ignorant, and inferior behavior by the enslaved African Americans, which was demoralizing. Two other examples of paternalism in the slave system were the illegitimacy of slave marriages and the frequent separation, by sale, of enslaved families.

Ogbu's racial identity theory

John Ogbu (2004) advanced the concept of collective identity, which refers to people's sense of belonging expressed through their beliefs, attitudes, and language. African Americans, a colonized minority group, experience this type of African American collective identity formation. Enslavement is an example of a collective experience (Ogbu, 1992). The oppression of enslavement, as a kind of African American "status problem," is a collective condition that is shared by African Americans in the United States. As a result of this shared condition, African Americans have responded collectively to the "status problem."

Ogbu (1992) examines African American identity formation from a historical context and contrasts the identity developments of involuntary and voluntary minority groups. Collective punishment and collective work contributed to the development of a new culture and new ways of speaking by enslaved African Americans. Before arriving in North America, enslaved Africans spoke a range of African languages and dialects. However, once enslaved, they were forced to learn the "American" language in order to survive. The enslaved, in turn, created their own forms of communication. During slavery, whites expected Blacks to behave in an ignorant or childlike manner. Whites demanded that Blacks act a certain way to exemplify inferiority. For example, learning to read or write was outlawed for slaves in this country. In response to these constraints, through this engrained and institutionalized culture, enslaved people developed an "oppositional" culture and their own forms of communication, in the form of religion, dialect, and song: they used coded lyrics, creating language patterns and codes that whites did not understand. For example, they used songs to communicate that danger or harm was nearby.

As a result, a dramatic shift took place in terms of American society's standard for Blacks to assimilate white American culture.

After emancipation, whites expected Blacks to speak and use the English language in the same manner as the "dominant culture." This was the only way Blacks could be viewed as "equals" in American society. This condition persists today as demonstrated in Ogbu's theory of "acting white." My parents advised me that, to be fully integrated and accepted by the "dominant" society, I must work twice as hard to assimilate through language acquisition because "standard English" speakers are viewed as more intelligent.

Ogbu (1992) argues that African Americans do not reject the achievement ideology of dominant American society and want to perform well academically in school. However, they reject certain behaviors that appear to suggest submission to the dominant culture. African Americans are viewed by some white Americans as inferior, which makes it difficult to cross the cultural divide between these two populations. Ogbu argues that the idea of African Americans not rejecting achievement ideology is based on culture. Society gives hidden messages about being smart and the correct way to behave in the education system. For example, in the schools that I attended, African American students were always underrepresented in advanced courses and overrepresented in basic courses. The institutions used tracking, language patterns, dress, and behavior as measures of academic standards. Schools still place African American students who are not perceived to follow the "dominant culture" in basic courses. These courses force them to comply with "what is expected" by the dominant culture. Holloway (2005) advanced this in his book *Africanisms in American Culture:*

For too long in this country whites have denied learning

from Blacks. That Black intellectual contributions have been slighted is only too obvious from the life stories of intellectual giants such as W.E.B. Du Bois. Many Blacks have had to hide their intelligence just to survive. The study of the legacy of African culture has an even greater obstacle to overcome in that many Blacks who were most adamant about being recognized for their contributions were most reluctant to claim African culture and most anxious to assimilate to European norms. To label something African was often a sure way to have it avoided by both Blacks and whites. An absurd example is the white southern claim to have invented the banjo.

(p. 376)

W. E. B. Du Bois

One key concept of African Americans' collective oppositional identity is that of "double consciousness." Coined by W. E. B. Du Bois, "double consciousness" describes how African Americans preserved a conscious Black identity in a white-dominated society (Moore, 2005). Du Bois, born in February 1868 during Reconstruction, is known by some as the father of American sociology. As a political activist, educator, and advocate for African people., he challenged the racial worldview through an Afrocentric paradigm that attempted to negate African Americans, as defined by his own African existence. Du Bois theorized that, to survive the American racial hierarchy, African Americans developed a "twoness"—a double consciousness—or a thought process of being "Negro" (i.e., Black) **and** American (i.e., non-Black). Du Bois placed the origin of "double consciousness" in a repressive culture that forces Blacks to see themselves through the eyes of the dominant white society (Moore, 2005). Akom (2008) summarized Du Bois's commentary on this idea of African American identity:

> Black personhood is existentially divided in at least two, perhaps more, selves—between the subjective, self-determined, agential self and the objectified, exoticized, excluded Other. These "existential" conditions created an additional sociopsychological condition that Du Bois named "twoness," an American, a Negro, two souls, two thoughts, two unreconciled strivings, two warring ideals in one dark body, whose dogged strength alone keeps it from being torn asunder.
>
> (p. 250)

"Twoness," according to Du Bois, is based on the belief that whites refuse to see African Americans as they are but see them as stereotypical projections of their minds. Blau and Brown (2001) highlighted Du Bois's thought that, thanks to double consciousness, Black people "have a profound understanding of the cultural frameworks and the institutional barriers that whites employ to oppress them" (p. 221).

Jointly, "twoness," "double consciousness," "acting white," and "code switching" are coping mechanisms to overcome racially oppressive North American social environments.

A theory of racism

Brondolo et al. (2012) assert that these three types of racism are multidimensional and can exert effects at the interpersonal level. The first type of racism is individual racism, where discrimination is expressed on a personal level. The second type of racism is institutional racism, which occurs when institutions and institutional policies exclude specific populations from participating fully in society. The third type of racism is cultural racism, by which the cultural practices of whites (the dominant group) are regarded as the norm and, therefore, superior. Brondolo et al. (2012) asserted that the term racism "can be manifest at the cultural, institutional, and individual levels, and can exert effects at the intrapersonal level" (p. 358).

By the twentieth century, the concept of biological racism had begun to lose ground. Owing to the socialist movement and new theories, such as individual, institutional, and cultural racism, the scientific discourse on the classification of human beings changed (Powell, 2000). African Americans had been viewed scientifically as "biologically inferior" to whites. As referenced in Chapter 2 of this book, the socialist movement challenged this theory by studying environmental conditions in cities and communities of color, as described by Du Bois (1899).

Prior to the civil rights era, institutional racism had been practiced not only in overt ways but most prevalently in covert ways (Speight, Vera, and Derrickson, 1996).

Institutional racism "refers to the ways in which racist beliefs or values have been built into the operations of social institutions in such a way as to discriminate against, control and oppress various minority groups" (Henry, Houston, and Mooney, 2004, p. 517). Institutional racism is embedded in American institutions of higher learning. Based on the literature about it, institutional racism is generally unrecognizable because it is largely covert. An individual may not be able to detect it because it is entrenched in the structures of society. Institutional racism refers to the specific policies and/or procedures of institutions (e.g., government, businesses, schools, churches) that consistently result in unequal treatment of particular groups (Better, 2002).

Individual racism is viewed as an individual bias that is an automatic or unconscious process and indirect expression of bias (McConahay, 1986). "Like institutional and cultural racism, individual prejudice is also commonly manifested subtly, often without conscious awareness or intention" (Romm, 2010, p. 71).

In the literature of sociology there is acknowledgment of various forms of individual racism. For example, overt or blatantly intentional forms of racism and subtle forms of racism can manifest in mistrusting personal relationships (Henkel, Dovidio, and Gaertner, 2006). Through stereotypes, grouping, prejudice, and discrimination, individual racism appears to be an expression of personal bias.

In the grand scheme of North American racism, the dominant racist theory of the early nineteenth century has roots in religion that, from 1850 to 1950, was rooted in natural science, and current racist theory is rooted in the history of culture (Blaut, 1992).

Cultural racism is defined as "societal beliefs and customs that promote the assumption that the products of white culture (i.e., language, traditions, appearance) are superior to those of nonwhite culture" (Helms, 1990, as cited in Powell, 2000, p. 8). The cultural superiority of Europeans or the "white race" is thought to be the effect of racial superiority. Cultural racism argues that non-Europeans are more culturally deprived than racially deprived, in comparison to Europeans, owing to a lack of cultural evolution that explains their impoverished condition. The belief is that non-Europeans must follow the cultural standards set forth by Europeans to be successful. Non-Europeans were considered to be members of inferior races, unable to achieve and to overcome cultural "backwardness." This position has been labeled "ethnocentrism."

During the era of classical and biological racism, it was believed that "the groundwork for cultural racism was laid by Max Weber and his theories on Modernization" (Young and Braziel, 2006, p. 79). Considered to be the "godfather" of cultural racism, Weber posited a theory of modernization based on the expansion of racist colonial ideology: a belief that the cultural history of Europeans is exclusive and superior. It emphasized "the uniqueness of the European mind—its rationality, its spiritual capacity—and historical argumentation about the unique rise within Europe, and Europe alone, of institutions and structures which were the source of modernity" (Blaut, 1992, p. 292).

Cultural history and its contributions to modernization and modern society became the standard by which the superiority of races was measured. Cultural superiority, in a manner of speaking, is based on a modern form of thinking in which non-Europeans are viewed less as racially inferior but more as culturally inferior to the white race owing to their historical background. Views about race are built primarily on racial stereotypes that are integral to sustaining an ideology of group differentiation and variation. Throughout history, cultural racism has been entrenched in the school system as seemingly moderate but actually is rooted in the ethnocentric standards of assimilation to white culture (Powell, 2000). In today's society, these perceptions can be influenced by the media's portrayal of African Americans on television (Punyanunt-Carter, 2008).

Cultural racism can apply to the manner in which individuals express their attitudes with regard to the "relative rights, privileges, and status that should be afforded to different racial/ ethnic groups"(Brondolo et al., 2012, p. 8). It can serve as a primary method for communicating stereotypes to racial and ethnic groups. This can influence social perceptions and ideologies of others.

Cultural racism usually functions at an unconscious level: people are often unaware of its operation and their behavior and attitudes. Normally, the term defines educational regulatory actions, yet one is often unaware of its implementation. Many white college students maintain firmly negative stereotypes about Blacks owing to their socialization prior to attending college.

Historically, cultural racism has been embedded in numerous educational practices based on the dominant worldview and behavioral standards of the dominant group (Brondolo et al., 2012). It is linked to ethnocentrism, or the tendency to judge other groups, societies, or lifestyles by the standards of one's own culture (Hooghe, 2008; Smith, 1991). When one group exerts the power to define the cultural values for society or when one group engages in ethnocentric behaviors toward other groups, then cultural racism ensues (Scott, 2007). The measure of cultural knowledge in the North American context is based on the cultural knowledge and conformity with the behavior of white Anglo-Saxon cultural practices. Of the three types of racism discussed here, cultural racism is the most intrinsically connected to the perpetuation of poor educational experiences of African Americans, particularly low-income African American students, whose cultural knowledge differs significantly from that of upper- and middle-class white populations (Powell, 2000).

Pierre Bourdieu

Pierre Bourdieu's theory of social reproduction is part of my explanatory model when analyzing the cultural value of enslaved Africans. The first concept of his theory of social reproduction is what he called *"habitus,"* which consists of the values and dispositions gained from cultural history that are carried throughout people's lives. Based on this theory, individual actions are determined by who the agent is, where the agent fits within a particular social structure, and the resources the agent has acquired from their social class status in society (McKnight and Chandler, 2012). For example, a person can obtain social, cultural, linguistic, and/or educational capital.

The second concept, "field," is the actual location or place where agents compete over resources that are of value, as determined by society. For example, race can be considered a field in Bordieuan terms, owing to its structural meaning, in that it denotes social stratification and levels of capital (McKnight and Chandler, 2012).

The third concept, "misrecognition," describes the ways in which people become complacent in their interactions. Both the oppressed and oppressor come to believe that their dominant or nondominant status is the natural order (McKnight and Chandler, 2012).

The fourth component of Bourdieu's theory of social reproduction, "symbolic violence," also known as "symbolic power" or "symbolic domination," is an integration of "*habitus*," "capital," "field," and "misrecognition" of the material structures and their subjective meanings in society (Bourdieu, Passeron and de Saint, 1996). According to McKnight and Chandler (2012), "Bourdieu integrates the material structures in society and the subjective meanings that social actors give to their experiences within those structures" (p. 77). In the United States, symbolic violence refers to the everyday unconscious actions by the group of those with power in American society toward African Americans in order to maintain that power structure and cultural domination. For example, race and gender discrimination can be viewed as symbolic violence (Bourdieu et al., 1996). This model provides a complex analysis to explain why social agents choose to act as they do. In his sociological analysis, Bourdieu used these concepts to examine why people from poor, middle-class, or affluent backgrounds perform certain actions and come to view those actions as natural and in conformity with cultural standards (Bourdieu and Passeron, 2000; Joppke, 1986). Bourdieu's explanatory model provides a framework to analyze the relationship between race and the social reproduction of cultural racism in the United States.

References

Akom, A. A. (2008). Black Metropolis and Mental Life: Beyond the "Burden of 'Acting White'" Toward a Third Wave of Critical Racial Studies. *Anthropology & Education Quarterly, 39*(3), pp. 247–265. www.jstor.org/stable/25166667

Alderman, C. L. (1975). *Colonists for Sale: The Story of Indentured Servants in America*. New York, NY: Macmillan.

Allen, A., Boxill, B., Hare, R. M. and Cohen, J. (1998). *Subjugation and Bondage: Critical Essays on Slavery and Social Philosophy*. Lanham, MD: Rowman & Littlefield.

Allen, R. L. (2005). Reassessing the Internal (Neo) Colonialism Theory. *The Black Scholar, 35*(1), pp. 2–11. https://doi.org/10.1080/00064246.2005.11413289

Allison, D., Cleveland, D., Foreman, D., Guzman, W. and Harewood, D. (2021). *Breaking Bias: Lessons from the Amistad*. New Brunswick, NJ: New Jersey State Bar Foundation.

Amira, K., Cooper, C. A., Knotts, H. G. and Wofford, C. (2018). The Southern Accent as a Heuristic in American Campaigns and Elections. *American Politics Research, 46*(6), pp. 1065–1093. https://doi.org/10.1177/1532673X18755655

Anderson, P. D. (2012). Supporting Caste: The Origins of Racism in Colonial Virginia. *Grand Valley Journal of History, 2*(1), p. 1. https://scholarworks.gvsu.edu/gvjh/vol2/iss1/1

Baker, L. D. (1998). *From Savage to Negro: Anthropology and the Construction of Race, 1896–1954*. Berkeley, CA: University of California Press.

Barstow, C. (2008). The Power Differential and the Power Paradox. *Hakomi Forum, 19*, pp. 20–21.

Baugh, J. (1999). *Out of the Mouths of Slaves: African American Language and Educational Malpractice.* Austin, TX: University of Texas Press.

Better, S. (2002). *Institutional Racism: A Primer on Theory and Strategies for Social Change.* Kingston upon Thames, UK: Burnham.

Blassingame, J. W. (1979). *The Slave Community* (Vol. 266). Oxford, UK: Oxford University Press.

Blatt, M. H. and Roediger, D. R. (eds.) (2018). *The Meaning of Slavery in the North.* New York, NY: Routledge.

Blau, J. R. and Brown, E. S. (2001). Du Bois and Diasporic Identity: The Veil and the Unveiling Project. *Sociological Theory, 19*(2), pp. 219–233. https://doi.org/10.1111/0735-2751.00137

Blauner, B. (2001). *Still the Big News: Racial Oppression in America.* Philadelphia, PA: Temple University Press.

Blauner, R. (1969). Internal Colonialism and Ghetto Revolt. *Social Problems, 16*(4), pp. 393–408. https://doi.org/10.2307/799949

Blaut, J. M. (1992). The Theory of Cultural Racism. *Antipode, 24*(4), pp. 289–299. https://doi.org/10.1111/j.1467-8330.1992.tb00448.x

Bogdanowicz, M., Burgelman, J. C., Collins, R., Curran, J., Gandy, O. H., Jr., Golding, P., Gourova, E., Hanada, T., Harvey, S., Horwitz, R., Javary, M., Mansell, R., McChesney, R., Miège, B., Mosco, V., Peters, J. D., Richeri, G., Streeter, T., Riordan, E. and Wasko, J. (2003). *Toward a Political Economy of Culture: Capitalism and Communication in the Twenty-first Century.* Lanham, MD: Rowman & Littlefield.

Bourdieu, P. and Passeron, J. C. (2000). *Language and Relationship to Language in the Teaching Situation.* Redwood City, CA: Stanford University Press.

Bourdieu, P., Passeron, J. C. and de Saint Martin, M. (1996). *Academic Discourse: Linguistic Misunderstanding and Professorial Power.* Redwood City, CA: Stanford University Press.

Brandt, A. M. (1978). Racism and Research: The Case of the Tuskegee Syphilis Study. *Hastings Center Report, 8*(6), pp. 21–29. http://nrs.harvard.edu/urn-3:HUL.InstRepos:3372911

Breitman, G. and Morrison, D. (1966). *How a Minority Can Change Society.* Allston, MA: Merit Publishers.

Brondolo, E., Libretti, M., Rivera, L. and Walsemann, K. M. (2012). Racism and Social Capital: The Implications for Social and Physical Well-being. *Journal of Social Issues, 68*(2), pp. 358–384. https://psycnet.apa.org/doi/10.1111/j.1540-4560.2012.01752.x

Brooks, W. M. and McNair, J. C. (2015). "Combing" through Representations of Black Girls' Hair in African American Children's Literature. *Children's Literature in Education, 46*(3), pp. 296–307. https://dx.doi.org/10.1007/s10583-014-9235-x

Brown, T. M. and de Casanova, E. M. (2014). Representing the Language of the "Other": African American Vernacular English in Ethnography. *Ethnography, 15*(2), pp. 208–231. www.jstor.org/stable/24467145

Bruner, E. M. (1996). Tourism in Ghana: The Representation of Slavery and the Return of the Black Diaspora. *American Anthropologist, 98*(2), pp. 290–304.

Byrd, A. and Tharps, L. (2014). *Hair Story: Untangling the Roots of Black Hair in America.* New York, NY: St. Martin's Press.

Cade, J. B. (1935). Out of the Mouths of Ex-slaves. *Journal of Negro History, 20*(3), pp. 294–337. https://doi.org/10.2307/2714721

Campbell, J. T. (2007). *Middle Passages: African American Journeys to Africa, 1787–2005.* New York, NY: The Penguin Press.

Casanova, P. G. (1965). Internal Colonialism and National Development. *Studies in Comparative International Development, 1*(4), pp. 27–37. https://doi.org/10.1007/BF02800542

Chase, G. (1970). *The Social Implications of Early Negro Music in the United States.* https://doi.org/10.2307/779935.

Clemens, P. G. (1975). The Operation of an Eighteenth-Century Chesapeake Tobacco Plantation. *Agricultural History*, pp. 517–531.

Cooley, H. S. (1896). *A Study of Slavery in New Jersey*. Baltimore, MD: Johns Hopkins Press.

Covey, H. C. (2007). *African American Slave Medicine: Herbal and Non-herbal Treatments*. Lanham, MD: Lexington Books.

Covey, H. C. and Eisnach, D. (2009). *What the Slaves Ate: Recollections of African American Foods and Foodways from the Slave Narratives*. Santa Barbara, CA: ABC-CLIO.

Cruse, H. W. (1960). *Revolutionary Nationalism and the Afro-American*. Indianapolis, IN: Bobbs-Merrill.

Cumming, I. P. (1959). Eatonton's Southern Accent. *The Georgia Review*, *13*(2), pp. 206–216. www.jstor.org/stable/41398153

Dennis, R. M. (1995). Social Darwinism, Scientific Racism, and the Metaphysics of Race. *Journal of Negro Education, 64,* pp. 243–252. https://doi.org/10.2307/2967206

Dillard, J. L. (1973). *Black English: Its History and Usage in the United States*. New York, NY: Vintage.

Du Bois, W. E. B. (1903). *The Souls of Black Folk*. Chicago, IL: McClurg.

Du Bois, W. E. B. and Eaton, I. (1899). *The Philadelphia Negro: A Social Study*. Philadelphia, PA: University of Pennsylvania.

Eisnach, D. and Covey, H. C. (2019). Slave Gardens in the Antebellum South: The Resolve of a Tormented People. *The Southern Quarterly, 57*(1), pp. 11–23.

Ekpenyonganwan. (2020). *The History of the Natural Hair of the African Community.* https://ng.opera.news/ng/en/fashion-bea uty/3b97bd5dbbb7496f2174da324a503eee

Farrison, W. E. (1977). *Lexicon of Black English*. New York, NY: Seabury Press.

Federal Writers' Project. (1936). Slave Narrative Project, Administrative Files [Manuscript/Mixed Material]. www.loc.gov/item/mesn001/

Fett, S. M. (2002). *Working Cures: Healing, Health, and Power on Southern Slave Plantations*. Chapel Hill, NC: University of North Carolina Press.

Finkelman, P. (ed.) (1989). *The Culture and Community of Slavery* (Vol. 8). New York, NY: Garland.

Fordham, S. and Ogbu, J. U. (1986). Black Students' School Success: Coping with the "Burden of 'Acting White.'" *The Urban Review, 18*(3), pp. 176–206.

Foreman, D. (2017). *W.E.B. Du Bois's Quest to Challenge Scientific Racism, 1906–1932: Educating the "City Negro" at the 135th Street Branch Library* (Doctoral dissertation, Rutgers University-Graduate School Newark). https://rucore.libraries.rutgers.edu/rutgers-lib/54112/

Forte, M. C. (2015). Encoding Poverty, Backwardness, and Dependency in US Military Imagery. https://zeroanthropology.net/2015/12/21/bare-feet/

Gehrmann, T. (2007). *African American English and White Southern English: Segregational Factors in the Development of a Dialect*. Munich, Germany: GRIN Verlag.

Gibbs, T., Cargill, K., Lieberman, L. S. and Reitz, E. (1980). Nutrition in a Slave Population: An Anthropological Examination. *Medical Anthropology, 4*(2), pp. 175–262. https://doi.org/10.1080/01459740.1980.9965868

Gibson, M. A. and Ogbu, J. U. (1991). *Minority Status and Schooling: A Comparative Study of Immigrant and Involuntary Minorities*. New York, NY: Garland.

Hammond, R. A. and Axelrod, R. (2006). The Evolution of Ethnocentrism. *Journal of Conflict Resolution, 50*(6), pp. 926–936. https://psycnet.apa.org/doi/10.1177/0022002706293470

Handler, J. S. (2000). Slave Medicine and Obeah in Barbados, circa 1650 to 1834. *New West Indian Guide, 74*(1–2), pp. 57–90. www.jstor.org/stable/41850026

Harper, C. W. (1985). Black Aristocrats: Domestic Servants on the Antebellum Plantation. *Phylon, 46*(2), pp. 123–135. https://doi.org/10.2307/274411

Hartzler-Miller, C. (2001). Making Sense of "Best Practice" in Teaching History. *Theory & Research in Social Education, 29*(4), pp. 672–695. https://doi.org/10.1080/00933104.2001.10505961

Healey, J. F. and O'Brien, E. (2014). *Race, Ethnicity, Gender, and Class: The Sociology of Group Conflict and Change.* Thousand Oaks, CA: Sage.

Healey, J. F., Stepnick, A. and O'Brien, E. (2018). *Race, Ethnicity, Gender, and Class: The Sociology of Group Conflict and Change.* Thousand Oaks, CA: Sage.

Henkel, K. E., Dovidio, J. F. and Gaertner, S. L. (2006). Institutional Discrimination, Individual Racism, and Hurricane Katrina. *Analyses of Social Issues and Public Policy, 6*(1), pp. 99–124. https://doi.org/10.1111/j.1530-2415.2006.00106.x

Henry, B. R., Houston, S. and Mooney, G. H. (2004). Institutional Racism in Australian Health Care: A Plea for Decency. *Medical Journal of Australia, 180*, pp. 517–520. PMID: 15139829

Herbert, R. (1970). *The Negro in the Tobacco Industry.* Philadelphia, PA: University of Pennsylvania Press.

Herskovits, M. J. (1938). *Acculturation: The Study of Culture Contact.* New York, NY: J. J. Augustin.

Hind, R. J. (1984). The Internal Colonial Concept. *Comparative Studies in Society and History, 26*, pp. 543–568. https://doi.org/10.1017/S0010417500011130

Holloway, J. (ed.) (2005). *Africanisms in American Culture.* Bloomington, IN: Indiana University Press.

Holloway, J. and Vass, W. K. (1997). *The African Heritage of American English*. Bloomington, IN: Indiana University Press.

Hooghe, M. (2008). *International Encyclopedia of the Social Sciences*. Farmington Hills, MI: MacMillan Reference.

Israel, A. M. (2018). Free Blacks, Quakers, and the Underground Railroad in Piedmont North Carolina. *North Carolina Historical Review, 95*(1), pp. 1–28. www.jstor.org/stable/45184905

Jim's Journey: The Huck Finn Freedom Center. (2022). Slave Narratives: Emma Knight. www.jimsjourney.org/slave-narratives

Johnson, W. (2000). The Slave Trader, the White Slave, and the Politics of Racial Determination in the 1850s. *Journal of American History, 87*(1), pp. 13–38. https://doi.org/10.2307/2567914

Jones, J. M. (1997). *Prejudice and Racism*. New York, NY: McGraw-Hill.

Joppke, C. (1986). The Cultural Dimensions of Class Formation and Class Struggle: On the Social Theory of Pierre Bourdieu. *Berkeley Journal of Sociology, 31*, pp. 53–78. Corpus ID: 141690108

Jordan, W. D. (1974). *The White Man's Burden: Historical Origins of Racism in the United States*. Oxford, UK: Oxford University Press.

Kendall, F. (2012). *Understanding White Privilege: Creating Pathways to Authentic Relationships across Race*. New York, NY: Routledge.

Kohn, M. (2005). Frederick Douglass's Master-Slave Dialectic. *The Journal of Politics, 67*(2), pp. 497–514. https://doi.org/10.1111/j.1468-2508.2005.00326.x

Kortright, C. (2003). Colonization and Identity. *The Anarchist Library*, 1–14. https://mirror.anarhija.net/lib.anarhija.net/mirror/c/ck/chris-kortright-colonization-and-identity.pdf

Kulikoff, A. (2012). *Tobacco and Slaves: The Development of Southern Cultures in the Chesapeake, 1680–1800*. Chapel Hill, NC: University of North Carolina Press.

Lanehart, S. L. (ed.) (2001). *Sociocultural and Historical Contexts of African American English*. Amsterdam, Netherlands: John Benjamins Publishing.

Lee, H. and Cho, Y. (2012). Introduction: Colonial Modernity and Beyond in East Asian Contexts. *Cultural Studies, 26*, pp. 601–616. https://doi.org/10.1080/09502386.2012.697702

Main, G. L. (2014). *Tobacco Colony: Life in Early Maryland, 1650–1720* (Vol. 651). Princeton, NJ: Princeton University Press.

McConahay, J. B. (1986). Modern Racism, Ambivalence, and the Modern Racism Scale. In J. F. Dovidio and S. L. Gaertner (eds.), *Prejudice, Discrimination, and Racism* (pp. 91–125). Cambridge, MA: Academic Press.

McGary, H. (1998). *Paternalism and Slavery, Subjugation and Bondage: Critical Essays on Slavery and Social Philosophy*. Lanham, MD: Rowman & Littlefield.

McKnight, D. and Chandler, P. (2012). The Complicated Conversation of Class and Race in Social and Curricular Analysis: An Examination of Pierre Bourdieu's Interpretative Framework in Relation to Race. *Educational Philosophy and Theory, 44*(S1), pp. 74–97. https://doi.org/10.1111/j.1469-5812.2009.00555.x

McManus, E. J. (2001a). *Black Bondage in the North*. Syracuse, NY: Syracuse University Press.

McManus, E. J. (2001b). *A History of Negro Slavery in New York*. Syracuse, NY: Syracuse University Press.

Memmi, A. (2013). *The Colonizer and the Colonized*. London, UK: Routledge.

Moore, F. (2009). *A History of the Black Church in Tuscaloosa*. Bloomington, IN: Author House.

Moore, T. O. (2005). A Fanonian Perspective on Double Consciousness. *Journal of Black Studies, 35*(6), pp. 751–762. www.jstor.org/stable/40034879

Morris, A. (2015). *The Scholar Denied: W.E.B. Du Bois and the Birth of Modern Sociology*. Berkeley, CA: University of California Press.

Mufwene, S. S. (2015). The Emergence of African American English: Monogenetic or Polygenetic? Under How Much Substrate Influence. In J. Bloomquist, L. J. Green and S. Lanehart (eds.), *The Oxford Handbook of African American Language* (pp. 57–84). Oxford, UK: Oxford University Press.

Noel, D. L. (1968). A Theory of the Origin of Ethnic Stratification. *Social Problems, 16*(2), pp. 157–172. https://doi.org/10.2307/800001

Northrup, H. R. (1970). *The Negro in the Tobacco Industry*. Philadelphia, PA: University of Pennsylvania Press.

Ntongela, N. (2009). The Historical and Literary Moment of Njabulo S. Ndebele. *English in Africa, 36*(1), pp. 17–39. www.jstor.org/stable/40239121

Ogbu, J. U. (1992). Adaptation to Minority Status and Impact on School Success. *Theory Into Practice, 31*(4), pp. 287–295. https://doi.org/10.1080/00405849209543555

Ogbu, J. U. (2004). Collective Identity and the Burden of "acting White" in Black History, Community, and Education. *The Urban Review, 36*(1), pp. 1–35. https://psycnet.apa.org/doi/10.1023/B:URRE.0000042734.83194.f6

Omi, M. and Winant, H. (2004). Racial Formations. *Race, Class, and Gender in the United States, 6*, 13–22.

Osofsky, G. (1966). *Harlem, the Making of a Ghetto: Negro New York, 1890–1930*. New York, NY: Harper & Row.

Otto, J. S. and Burns, A. M. (1983). Black Folks and Poor Buckras: Archeological Evidence of Slave and Overseer Living Conditions on an Antebellum Plantation. *Journal of Black Studies, 14*(2), pp. 185–200. www.jstor.org/stable/2784318

Pollitzer, W. S. (1999). *The Gullah People and Their African Heritage*. Athens, GA: University of Georgia Press.

Powell, R. (2000). Overcoming Cultural Racism: The Promise of Multicultural Education. *Multicultural Perspectives, 2*(3), pp. 8–14. https://doi.org/10.1207/S15327892MCP0203_03

Prayag, G., Suntikul, W. and Agyeiwaah, E. (2018). Domestic Tourists to Elmina Castle, Ghana: Motivation, Tourism Impacts, Place Attachment, and Satisfaction. *Journal of Sustainable Tourism, 26*(12), pp. 2053–2070. https://doi.org/10.1080/09669 582.2018.1529769

Price, J. M. (1956). The Beginnings of Tobacco Manufacture in Virginia. *Virginia Magazine of History and Biography, 64*(1), pp. 3–29. www.jstor.org/stable/4246193

Price, J. M. (1964). The Economic Growth of the Chesapeake and the European Market, 1697–1775. *Journal of Economic History, 24*(4), pp. 496–511. https://doi.org/10.1017/S0022050700061210

Punyanunt-Carter, N. M. (2008). The Perceived Realism of African American Portrayals on Television. *Howard Journal of Communications, 19*(3), pp. 241–257. https://doi.org/10.1080/10646170802218263

Reinhard, W. (2001). History of Colonization and Colonialism. *International Encyclopedia of the Social and Behavioral Sciences,* pp. 2240–2245.

Rodriguez, C. (2003). Hair Story: Untangling the Roots of Black Hair in America. *Transforming Anthropology, 11*(2), pp. 64–65. https://doi.org/10.1525/tran.2003.11.2.64

Romm, N. (2010). *New Racism: Revisiting Researcher Accountabilities.* Berlin, Germany: Springer Science & Business Media.

Schaffer, M. (2005). Bound to Africa: The Mandinka Legacy in the New World. *History in Africa, 32*, pp. 321–369. www.jstor.org/sta ble/20065748

Scott, C. L. (2007). A Discussion of Individual, Institutional, and Cultural Racism, with Implications for HRD. http://files.eric. ed.gov/fulltext/ED504856.pdf

Smedley, A. (1998). "Race" and the Construction of Human Identity. *American Anthropologist, 100*, pp. 690–702. www.jstor.org/stable/682047

Smedley, B. D. and Smedley, A. (2012). *Race in North America: Origin and Evolution of a Worldview*. New York, NY: Avalon Publishing.

Smith, E. J. (1991). Ethnic Identity Development: Toward the Development of a Theory within the Context of Majority/Minority Status. *Journal of Counseling and Development, 70*(1), pp. 181–188. https://psycnet.apa.org/doi/10.1002/j.1556-6676.1991.tb01581.x

Sousa, E. C. and Raizada, M. N. (2020). Contributions of African Crops to American Culture and Beyond: The Slave Trade and Other Journeys of Resilient Peoples and Crops. *Frontiers in Sustainable Food Systems, 4*, p. 586340. https://doi.org/10.3389/fsufs.2020.586340

Speight, S. L., Vera, E. M. and Derrickson, K. B. (1996). Racial Self-designation, Racial Identity, and Self-esteem Revisited. *Journal of Black Psychology, 22*(1), pp. 37–52. https://psycnet.apa.org/doi/10.1177/00957984960221004

Vogan, C. (2022). The History of Hula Hooping: From 500 BCE to the 21st Century. www.hulahooping.com/history.html

Wagley, C. and Harris, M. (1958). *Minorities in the New World*. New York, NY: Columbia University Press.

Walker, S. S. (2001). *African Roots/American Cultures*. Lanham, MD: Rowman & Littlefield.

Washington, B. T. (1899). *The Future of the American Negro*. New York, NY: Negro Universities Press.

Westmacott, R. N. (1992). *African-American Gardens and Yards in the Rural South*. Knoxville, TN: University of Tennessee Press.

White, S. and White, G. (1995a). Slave Clothing and African-American Culture in the Eighteenth and Nineteenth Centuries. *Past & Present, 148*, pp. 149–186. www.jstor.org/stable/651051

White, S. and White, G. (1995b). Slave Hair and African American Culture in the Eighteenth and Nineteenth Centuries. *Journal of Southern History, 61*(1), pp. 45–76. https://doi.org/10.2307/2211360

Young, J. A. and Braziel, J. E. (eds.) (2006). *Race and the Foundations of Knowledge: Cultural Amnesia in the Academy*. Champaign, IL: University of Illinois Press.

Recommended further reading

Adelman, L., Pounder, C., Herbes-Sommers, C., Strain, T. H., Smith, L. M. and Enhance, T. (2003). *Race: The Power of an Illusion* [Newsreel]. California Newsreel.

Anyon, J. (1997). *Ghetto Schooling: A Political Economy of Urban Educational Reform*. New York, NY: Teachers College Press.

Anyon, J. (2012). *Schools and Poverty*. New York, NY: Teachers College of Columbia University.

Anyon, J. (2014). *Radical Possibilities: Public Policy, Urban Education, and a New Social Movement*. New York, NY: Routledge.

Armour, A. W. (1941). *The Negro in Virginia*. New York, NY: Hastings House.

Asante, M. K., Brandon, G., Hall, R. L., Gaston, J. R., Maultsby, P. K., Philip, J. E. and Williams, S. W. (2005). *Africanisms in American Culture*. Bloomington, IL: Indiana University Press.

Ashe, B. D. (1995). "Why don't he like my hair?" Constructing African-American Standards of Beauty in Toni Morrison's *Song of Solomon* and Zora Neale Hurston's *Their Eyes Were Watching God*. *African American Review*, *29*(4), pp. 579–592.

Bailey, G. (2002). Real and Apparent Time. In J. K. Chambers, P. Trudgill, and N. Schilling-Estes (eds.), *The Handbook of Language Variation and Change*, (pp. 312–331). Malden, MA: Blackwell

Baker, C. R., Colbert, S. D., Dubey, M., Knight, N., Ndounou, M. W., Nishikawa, K., Pinto, S. and Woolfork, L. (2019). *Black Cultural*

Production after Civil Rights. Champaign, IL: University of Illinois Press.

Baldwin, J., Capouya, E., Hansberry, L., Hentoff, N., Hughes, L. and Kazin, A. (1961). The Negro in American Culture. *CrossCurrents, 11*(3), pp. 205–224. www.jstor.org/stable/24456864

Barkan, E. R. (2012). *Immigrants in American History: Arrival, Adaptation, and Integration*. Santa Barbara, CA: ABC-CLIO.

Bascom, W. R. (1992). *African Folktales in the New World*. Bloomington, IN: Indiana University Press.

Beale, H. K. (1934). The Needs of Negro Education in the United States. *Journal of Negro Education, 3,* pp. 8–19.

Benedict, R. (1942). *Race and Racism*. New York, NY: Routledge.

Benson, P. (2012). *Tobacco Capitalism: Growers, Migrant Workers, and the Changing Face of a Global Industry*. Princeton, NJ: Princeton University Press.

Bernstein, B. B. (2003). *Class, Codes and Control: Applied Studies Towards a Sociology of Language* (Vol. 2). New York, NY: Routledge.

Bishop, R. S. (2011). African American Children's Literature. In S. Wolf, K. Coats, P. Enciso and C. Jenkins (eds.), *Handbook of Research on Children's and Young Adult Literature* (pp. 225–236). New York, NY: Routledge.

Blauner, B. (1972). *Racial Oppression in America*. New York, NY: HarperCollins College Division.

Bonilla-Silva, E. (1997). Rethinking Racism: Toward a Structural Interpretation. *American Sociological Review, 62,* pp. 465–480. https://doi.org/10.2307/2657316

Brotz, H. and Austin, B. W. (1992). *African-American Social and Political Thought, 1850–1920*. Piscataway, NJ: Transaction Publishers. [Previous ed. published under title *Negro social and political thought, 1850–1920*, 1966.]

Buhler-Wilkerson, K. (1993). Bringing Care to the People: Lillian Wald's Legacy to Public Health Nursing. *American Journal of Public Health, 83*, pp. 1778–1786. https://doi.org/10.2105%2Fajph.83.12.1778

Burke, C. S. and Castaneda, C. J. (2007). The Public and Private History of Eugenics: An Introduction. *The Public Historian, 20*(3), pp. 5–17.

Butcher, M. J. (1972). *The Negro in American Culture*. New York, NY: Knopf.

Childs, M. D. (2010). Slave Culture. In G. Heuman and T. Burnard (eds.), *The Routledge History of Slavery* (pp. 170–186). New York, NY: Routledge.

Cimino, E. C. (2012). *On the "Border Line of Tragedy": White Slavery, Moral Protection, and the Travelers' Aid Society of New York, 1885–1917* (Publication No. 3540112) Doctoral dissertation, Molloy College. ProQuest Dissertations and Theses Global.

Clark, K. B. (1989). *Dark Ghetto: Dilemmas of Social Power*. Middletown, CT: Wesleyan University Press.

Coffin, T. P. (1922). *Folklore in America: Tales, Songs, Superstitions, Proverbs, Riddles, Games, Folk Drama and Folk Festivals*. New York, NY: Doubleday.

Cusick, H. H. (1995). *Soul and Spice: African Cooking in the Americas*. San Francisco, CA: Chronicle Books.

Dillard, J. L. (1975). *Perspectives on Black English*. The Hague Mouton.

Donald, H. H. (1921). *The Negro Migration of 1916–1918*. Washington, DC: Association for the Study of Negro Life and History.

Dovidio, J. F. and Gaertner, S. L. (2004). Aversive Racism. *Advances in Experimental Social Psychology, 36*, pp. 1–52. https://psycnet.apa.org/doi/10.1016/S0065-2601(04)36001-6

Draper, E. S. (1932). Southern Plantations. *Landscape Architecture, 23*(1), pp. 1–14. www.jstor.org/stable/i40195108

Du Bois, W. E. B. (1959). *The History of Africa*. Amherst, MA: University of Massachusetts Amherst Libraries.

Eyerman, R. (2001). *Cultural Trauma: Slavery and the Formation of African American Identity*. Cambridge: Cambridge University Press.

Feagin, J. R. and Sikes, M. P. (1995). How Black Students Cope with Racism on White Campuses. *Journal of Blacks in Higher Education, 8*, pp. 91–97. www.jstor.org/stable/2963064

Foner, E. (ed.) (1970). *America's Black Past: A Reader in Afro-American History*. New York, NY: Harper & Row.

Fortier, P. A. (1967). Gobineau and German Racism. *Comparative Literature, 19*, pp. 341–350. https://doi.org/10.2307/1769493

Gikandi, S. (2011). *Slavery and the Culture of Taste*. Princeton, NJ: Princeton University Press.

Greenberg, J. H. (1970). *The Languages of Africa*. Bloomington, IN: Indiana University Press.

Grégoire, H., Cassirer, T. and Brière, J.-F. (1996). *On the Cultural Achievements of Negroes*. Amherst, MA: University of Massachusetts Press.

Guess, T. J. (2006). The Social Construction of Whiteness: Racism by Intent, Racism by Consequence. *Critical Sociology, 32*, pp. 649–673. https://doi.org/10.1163/156916306779155199

Halliday, R. J. (1971). Social Darwinism: A Definition. *Victorian Studies, 14*, pp. 389–405. www.jstor.org/stable/3825958

Harris, J. B. (2011). *High on the Hog: A Culinary Journey from Africa to America*. London, UK: Bloomsbury.

Hasian, M. A. (1996). *The Rhetoric of Eugenics in Anglo-American thought*. Athens, GA: University of Georgia Press.

Helms, J. E. (1990). *Black and White Racial Identity: Theory, Research, and Practice.* Westport, CT: Greenwood Press.

Herskovits, M. J. (1958). *Acculturation: The Study of Culture Contact.* New York, NY: J. J. Augustin.

Herskovits, M. J. (1962). *The Human Factor in Changing Africa.* New York, NY: Knopf.

Herskovits, M. J. (1966). *The New World Negro.* Indianapolis, IN: Indiana University Press.

Herskovits, M. J. (1990). *The Myth of the Negro Past.* Boston, MA: Beacon Press.

Herskovits, M. J. (2013). *The Human Factor in Changing Africa.* New York, NY: Routledge.

Hilliard, S. B. (1972). *Hogmeat and Hoecake: Food Supply in the Old South, 1840–1860.* Carbondale, IL: Southern Illinois University Press.

Hirschman, C. (1983). America's Melting Pot Reconsidered. *Annual Review of Sociology, 9,* pp. 397–423.

Holloway, J. and Keppel, B. (eds.) (2007). *Black Scholars on the Line: Race, Social Science, and American Thought in the Twentieth Century.* Notre Dame, IN: University of Notre Dame Press.

Hudson, N. (1996). From "Nation" to "Race": The Origin of Racial Classification in Eighteenth-century Thought. *Eighteenth-Century Studies, 29,* pp. 247–264. www.jstor.org/stable/30053821

Jablokow, V. R. (1956). Carl von Linne. *Canadian Medical Association Journal, 74*(12), pp. 1009–1010. www.ncbi.nlm.nih.gov/pmc/articles/pmc1824469/

Joyner, C. W. (1999). *Shared Traditions: Southern History and Folk Culture.* Champaign, IL: University of Illinois Press.

Kaestle, C. F. (1973). *The Evolution of an Urban School System: New York City, 1750–1850.* Cambridge, MA: Harvard University Press.

Kalaidjian, W. B. (1993). *American Culture between the Wars: Revisionary Modernism and Postmodern Critique*. New York, NY: Columbia University Press.

Katz, B. (1969). *The Social Implications of Early Negro Music in the United States*. New York, NY: Arno Press.

Kendall, D. (2012). *Sociology in Our Times*. Boston, MA: Cengage Learning.

Klineberg, O. (1944). *Characteristics of the American Negro*. New York, NY: Harper & Row.

Laidlaw, W. (1932). Population of the City of New York, 1890–1930. www.census.gov/popuation/www/documentation/twps0076/twps0076.html

Lanehart, S. L. (ed.) (2015). *The Oxford Handbook of African American Language*. Oxford, UK: Oxford University Press.

Larson, J. L. (1967). Linnaeus and the Natural Method. *Isis, 58,* pp. 304–320. https://doi.org/10.1086/350265

Lemann, N. (2011). *The Promised Land: The Great Black Migration and How It Changed America*. New York, NY: Vintage.

Levine, L. W. (2007). *Black Culture and Black Consciousness: Afro-American Folk Thought from Slavery to Freedom* (Vol. 530). Oxford, UK: Oxford University Press.

Linné, C. (1997). The God-given Order of Nature. In E. Chuckwudi (ed.), *Race and the Enlightenment: A Reader* (pp. 10–14). Hoboken, NJ: Blackwell.

Lowance, M. I., Jr. (ed.). (2018). *A House Divided: The Antebellum Slavery Debates in America, 1776–1865*. Princeton, NJ: Princeton University Press.

MacLeod, J. (2009). *Ain't no Makin' It: Aspirations and Attainment in a Low-Income Neighborhood*. Boulder, CO: Westview Press.

Maddox, K. B. (2006). *Rethinking Racial Stereotyping, Prejudice, and Discrimination*. American Psychological Association.

Margo, R. A. and Steckel, R. H. (1982). The Heights of American Slaves: New Evidence on Slave Nutrition and Health. *Social Science History*, *6*(4), pp. 516–538. https://doi.org/10.2307/1170974

Matsuda, M. J. (1991). Voices of America: Accent, Antidiscrimination Law, and a Jurisprudence for the Last Reconstruction. *Yale Law Journal*, *100*(5), pp. 1329–1407. https://doi.org/10.2307/796694

McCullough Buschle, C. (2010). Uncovering the History of the Hula Hoop. www.wired.com/2010/11/uncovering-the-history-of-the-hula-hoop/

Michael, D. B. (1970). *Father of Racist Ideology*. London, UK: Weidenfeld & Nicolson.

Montgomery, W. E. (1975). *Negro Churches in the South, 1865–1915*. Austin, TX: The University of Texas at Austin.

Moore, J. M. (2003). *Booker T. Washington, WEB Du Bois, and the Struggle for Racial Uplift*. Lanham, MD: Rowman & Littlefield.

Morsman, A. F. (2010). *The Big House after Slavery: Virginia Plantation Families and Their Postbellum Domestic Experiment*. Charlottesville, VA: University of Virginia Press.

Olmsted, F. L. (1860) (1971). *The Cotton Kingdom: A Selection*. Edited by David F. Hawke. Indianapolis, IN: Bobbs-Merrill

Otto, J. S. (1977). Artifacts and Status Differences—A Comparison of Ceramics from Planter, Overseer, and Slave Sites on an Antebellum Plantation, In S. South (ed.), *Research Strategies in Historical Archaeology* (pp. 91–118), New York, NY: Academic Press.

Palmié, S. (1995). *Slave Cultures and the Cultures of Slavery*. Knoxville, TN: University of Tennessee Press.

Poplack, S. (ed.) (2000). *The English History of African American English*. Hoboken, NJ: Blackwell.

Quraishi, M. and Philburn, R. (2015). *Researching Racism: A Guidebook for Academics and Professional Investigators*. Thousand Oaks, CA: Sage.

Rawley, J. A. (1991a). Richard Harris, Slave Trader Spokesman. *Albion, 23*(3), pp. 439–458.

Rawley, J. A. (1991b). Slave Trade. In E. Foner and J. A. Garraty (eds.), *The Reader's Companion to American History* (pp. 994–995). Boston, MA: Houghton Mifflin.

Ritvo, H. (2009). Humans and Humanists. *Daedalus, 138*(3), pp. 68–78. http://hdl.handle.net/1721.1/56005

Samford, P. (1996). The Archaeology of African-American Slavery and Material Culture. *The William and Mary Quarterly, 53*, pp. 87–114.

Schomburg, A. A. (1925). The Negro Digs Up His Past. *Atheneum, 1975*, pp. 231–233.

Sears, D. O. and Henry, P. J. (2003). The Origins of Symbolic Racism. *Journal of Personality and Social Psychology, 85*(2), pp. 259–267. https://psycnet.apa.org/doi/10.1037/0022-3514.85.2.259

Silkenat, D. (2021). *Scars on the Land: An Environmental History of Slavery in the American South*. Oxford, UK: Oxford University Press.

Simpson, G. E. and Herskovits, M. (1973). *Selections from the Writings of Melville J. Herskovits, 1895–1963*. New York, NY: Columbia University Press.

Smedley, A. and Smedley, B. D. (2005). Race as Biology Is Fiction, Racism as a Social Problem Is Real: Anthropological and Historical Perspectives on the Social Construction of Race. *American Psychologist, 60*(1), pp. 16–29. https://psycnet.apa.org/doi/10.1037/0003-066X.60.1.16

Smith, L. [Director]. (2009). *Herskovits at the Heart of Blackness* [Newsreel]. Independent Lens.

Sternberg, R. J., Grigorenko, E. L. and Kidd, K. K. (2005). Intelligence, Race, and Genetics. *American Psychologist*, 60(1), pp. 46–62. https://psycnet.apa.org/doi/10.1037/0003-066X.60.1.46

Stuurman, S. (2000). François Bernier and the Invention of Racial Classification. *History Workshop Journal, 50*, pp. 1–21. www.jstor.org/stable/4289688

Taylor, J. G. (1982). Eating, Drinking, and Visiting in the South: An Informal History. Baton Rouge, LA: Louisiana State University Press.

Thai, T. (2022). The Surprisingly Long History of Hula Hoops. www.britannica.com/reviews/hula-hoop-history

Thomas, E. R. and Carter, P. M. (2006). Prosodic Rhythm and African American English. *English World-Wide, 27*(3), pp. 331–355. www.lib.ncsu.edu/resolver/1840.2/2063

Uhai Haircare. (2020). The History of Hair in the African American Community.   https://uhaihair.com/blogs/news/hair-history-a-short-story-on-the-evolution-of-hair-in-the-african-american-community

Weatherford, W. D. (1957). American Churches and the Negro: An Historical Study from Early Slave Days to the Present. *Archives de Sciences Sociales des Religions, 7*(1), pp. 190–190.

Winant, H. (2004). Race: The Power of an Illusion. www.pbs.org/race/000_General/000_00-Home.htm

Woolfork, L. (2019). *Black Cultural Production after Civil Rights*. Champaign, IL: University of Illinois Press.

Work, J. W. (1969). *Folk Song of the American Negro*. New York, NY: Negro Universities Press.

Worth, R. (2016). *Life as a Slave*. Berkeley Heights, NJ: Enslow.

Yentsch, A. E. (2007). Excavating the South's African American Food History. In A. L. Bower (ed.), *African American Foodways:*

Explorations of History and Culture, (pp. 59–98). Urbana: University of Illinois Press.

Young, R. J. (2015). *Empire, Colony, Postcolony*. New York, NY: Wiley.

Zeigler, M. B. and Osinubi, V. (2002). Theorizing the Postcoloniality of African American English. *Journal of Black Studies*, *32*(5), pp. 588–609. www.jstor.org/stable/3180954

Index

www.ingramcontent.com/pod-product-compliance
Lightning Source LLC
Chambersburg PA
CBHW070346270326
41926CB00017B/4006